ISAIAH

WESLEY BIBLE STUDIES

wesleyan
PUBLISHING HOUSE
wphstore.com

CONTENTS

INTRODUCTION

Good News! Bad News!

An art gallery owner told an artist, "I have good news and bad news."

The artist asked, "What's the good news?"

"The good news," the gallery owner replied, "is that a man visited the gallery yesterday and asked if the value of your paintings will increase after you die. When I told him it would, he bought all your paintings."

"That's great," the artist replied, but what's the bad news?"

The gallery owner hung his head. "That man was your doctor."

The book of Isaiah contains both good news and bad news, but the prophet delivered bad news first.

FIRST, THE BAD NEWS

Israel was far from God when Isaiah prophesied. Although they were going through the motions of religion, they were leading sinful lives. According to Isaiah 1, there was no soundness in them. They had rebelled against God, and they were perpetrating injustices. Consequently, their country was desolate and ravaged by foreigners. Further, their long-reigning king had died. Israel needed to repent and start doing what was right in God's sight.

But Isaiah caught sight of the exalted King of the universe, and when he saw God's intrinsic holiness, he also saw his own sinfulness. Although he was a prophet, his lips were unclean. Isaiah needed to be cleansed before he declared God's message.

The Gentile nations also received bad news. God would judge them. Assyria, Moab, Egypt, and Babylon would feel the heavy weight of His judgment. Indeed, the theme of judgment dominates the first half of the book of Isaiah (chs. 1–39).

NOW, THE GOOD NEWS

God does not delight in judgment. Even in the midst of Isaiah's negative pronouncements, he shared outstanding good news: A virgin would conceive and bear a son. His name would be Immanuel, meaning "God with us." He would bring forgiveness and restoration, and He would rule the nations. Hope in the coming Redeemer would replace despair with peace and sadness with joy.

Good news dominates the second half of Isaiah (chs. 40–66). God offered to comfort His people, and He invited all the ends of the earth to turn to Him and be saved (Isa. 45:22). Thirsty souls are urged to come to the waters and quench their thirst free of charge (55:1).

But there is even more good news: Someday, the Redeemer will restore the earth to Edenic conditions. Peace and joy will fill the hearts of earth's inhabitants.

On what basis does this good news rest? Isaiah 53 points to Jesus, the Lamb of God, as making reconciliation with God and peace and joy possible. "We all, like sheep, have gone astray, each of us has turned to his own way; and the LORD has laid on him the iniquity of us all" (v. 6).

Expect your joy to overflow as you pursue this study of Isaiah.

1

GOD'S REMEDY FOR REBELLION

Isaiah 1:1–9, 18–20

God has a heart for His people.

When the Welsh revival swept across Wales, a gentleman traveled from London to observe the phenomenon. Upon detraining at a village in Wales, he walked to the little community's square, where he approached a policeman. "Sir," he asked the policeman, "can you tell where the Welsh revival is taking place?"

Placing a finger on his uniform's copper buttons, the policeman answered, "The Welsh revival, Sir, is under these buttons."

Isaiah called upon Israel to undergo a revival. God was offering cleansing and forgiveness to all who would turn aside from rebellion and religious hypocrisy and come to Him. God's people can experience a similar revival today.

COMMENTARY

Isaiah ministered from 740 B.C. to approximately 681 B.C. His messages often relayed a warning of God's judgment upon His people because of their sins. Yet he was willing to endure rejection and persecution in order to be God's mouthpiece.

Isaiah prophesied during the period of the divided kingdom. The original nation of Israel had split in two. The southern kingdom, which was made up of the tribes of Judah and Benjamin, was referred to as Judah. The northern kingdom made up of all the other ten tribes was referred to as Israel. In the book of Isaiah, *Israel* sometimes refers to this northern kingdom, but in other places it refers to a united kingdom of all God's chosen people.

Carefully examining the context of each passage is crucial in determining which group of people is being referenced.

The northern kingdom had greatly sinned against God. They had no godly kings, so, consequently, they had turned to worshiping idols and oppressing the helpless. They were also compromising their call as God's people by entering into military alliances with pagan nations. Finally, in 722 B.C., the northern kingdom of Israel was carried into captivity by the Assyrians. Isaiah lived to see the fulfillment of this prophecy.

The southern kingdom was also forsaking the God of their fathers. They would be taken captive by the Babylonians, who would finally destroy Jerusalem and the temple in 586 B.C. Isaiah predicted this event but did not live to see it.

The book of Isaiah is divided into two major sections. The first section (chs. 1–39) is a collection of prophetic judgments against Judah, Israel, and the Gentile nations. The second part of the book (chs. 40–66) is what some have called the "book of comfort." Herein are contained the prophecies of the fall of Babylon, the restoration of Israel as a nation, and the coming of the Messiah, as well as the promise of God's everlasting kingdom.

Introducing the Prophet Isaiah (Isa. 1:1)

The book of Isaiah begins with a group of prophecies (chs. 1–5) that reflect the purpose of the whole book.

In this first verse, Isaiah identified himself and his times. The name Isaiah means "the Lord is salvation." It has been suggested that Isaiah's father, Amoz, might have been King Uzziah's uncle. If so, then Isaiah was of royal descent.

Isaiah prophesied **during the reigns of Uzziah, Jotham, Ahaz and Hezekiah,** all **kings of Judah** (1:1). His ministry spanned approximately sixty years. And through all these years, he sought to faithfully give each of these kings God's message.

WORDS FROM WESLEY

Isaiah 1:1

Vision—Or, the visions; the word being here collectively used: the sense is, this is the book of the visions or prophecies. As prophets were called Seers, 1 Sam. 9:9, so prophecies are called visions, because they were as clearly and certainly represented to the prophets minds, as bodily objects are to men's eyes. *Saw*—Foresaw and foretold. But he speaks, after the manner of the prophets, of things to come, as if they were either past or present. *Judah*—Principally, but not exclusively. For he prophecies also concerning Egypt and Babylon, and divers other countries; yet with respect to Judah. *The days*—In the time of their reign. Whence it may be gathered, that Isaiah exercised his prophetical office above fifty years together. (ENOT)

God's Evaluation of His Children (Isa. 1:2–4)

Some have suggested that chapter 1 is the whole book of Isaiah in a nutshell. It begins with God's evaluation of the sinful state of His people.

Hear, O heavens! Listen, O earth! For the Lord has spoken (v. 2). In the law of Moses, two witnesses were required to convict someone of a crime (see Deut. 9:15). When God established His covenant with His people, He called upon the heavens and earth to testify that the nation of Israel had promised to obey all the conditions of this covenant (see Deut. 31:28). Once again, God was calling on heaven and earth as the two witnesses to what He was about to say.

The Lord declared to them, **"I reared children and brought them up, but they have rebelled against me"** (Isa. 1:2). The word picture here helps us understand the emotion behind this message. God was like a faithful father who had reared His children in the way of holiness and then saw those children turn away and reject Him completely.

The people were totally ungrateful to God for all He had done for them. **The ox knows his master, the donkey his**

owner's manager, but Israel does not know, my people do not understand (v. 3). In other words, even the beasts have more sense than to turn from the one who is able to take care of them.

WORDS FROM WESLEY
Isaiah 1:3

Know—Me their owner and master. Knowing is here taken practically, as it is usually in Scripture, and includes reverence and obedience. (ENOT)

The sinful state of God's people is further described in verse 4. They are referred to as a **sinful nation, a people loaded with guilt, a brood of evildoers,** and those **given to corruption**. They are further described as those who **have spurned the Holy One of Israel** by turning **their backs on him**.

Today, God still looks at those He has created—both believer and unbeliever alike. He evaluates us all and, therefore, calls for us to evaluate ourselves. How many different ways have we turned our backs to the One who is only working out that which is perfect in our lives? How many times have we relied on human power and reasoning rather than the perfect knowledge of God? In doing so, we are no better than those Jews who had turned their backs on God.

The Results of Rebellion (Isa. 1:5–9)

The beginning of this paragraph poses questions: **Why should you be beaten anymore? Why do you persist in rebellion?** (v. 5). In other words, their sinful state did not make any sense. They were reaping the results of their willful rejection of God.

That sin's effect was catastrophic can be seen in the statement: **Your whole head is injured** (v. 5). Sin affects the way we think.

It affects our philosophy of life. Our minds control what we do; therefore, when we think wrong, we do wrong. Our bent on wanting to understand everything can keep us from following God by faith. Our finite minds cannot comprehend the ways of an infinite God. His ways can only be understood through faith.

That sin's effects could not be contained is seen in the next statement: **Your whole heart afflicted** (v. 5). Sin doesn't infiltrate just a small section of our hearts; it comes in and takes over. The **heart** in Scripture is a metaphor for the deepest part of who we are. Sin affects the very core of our being. That is why we cannot adequately deal with our own sin. Only Jesus, who knew no sin, could be our substitute sacrifice. When we entertain a little sin, we eventually find that our whole being is affected.

From the sole of your foot to the top of your head there is no soundness—only wounds and welts and open sores (v. 6). If Israel were to be pictured as a body, no part of it could be pronounced healthy. Everywhere one looked, sin had ravaged it.

WORDS FROM WESLEY

Isaiah 1:7

In your presence—Which your eyes shall see to torment you, when there is no power in your hands to deliver you. *As*—Heb. *as the overthrow of strangers*, that is, which strangers bring upon a land which is not likely to continue in their hands, and therefore they spare no persons, and spoil and destroy all things, which is not usually done in wars between persons of the same, or of a neighbouring nation. (ENOT)

Your country is desolate, your cities burned with fire; your fields are being stripped by foreigners right before you (v. 7). Isaiah predicted the desolation that was to come to the land God had given them. Assyria would devastate most of the country in 701 B.C., and then Babylon would finish the job in

605 B.C. The same land God had promised to them in covenant (Gen. 15:18–21) was about to be taken from them as a result of their sin.

The term **Daughter of Zion** in Isaiah 1:8 refers to Israel. The mount upon which Jerusalem was built was called Zion. Israel is often portrayed as a young woman in Scripture. In verse 8, **the Daughter of Zion** is compared to a **shelter in a vineyard, like a hut in a field of melons**. The picture here is of the huts or temporary shelters that were built during times of harvest. The people would live in these huts in order to watch for thieves and to keep animals away. After the harvest, the huts were abandoned and eventually destroyed. This is what was about to happen to the nation of Israel.

Unless the LORD Almighty had left us some survivors, we would have become like Sodom, we would have been like Gomorrah (v. 9). **LORD Almighty** refers to God's sovereignty over all of heaven and earth. Unless the One who is Lord of everything would intervene, Israel would be utterly destroyed like Sodom and Gomorrah. The severity of Israel's sin is seen in this comparison of Israel to Sodom and Gomorrah—cities of the hated and pagan Gentiles.

God had promised the land to Israel as part of His covenant with them, yet their sin caused it to be torn from them and destroyed before their eyes. Our sin can cause the very thing that God wants to give us to be taken from us. Sin blocks God's hand of blessing and keeps us from experiencing all God has for us.

God's Remedy for Israel's Sin (Isa. 1:18–20)

God's desire was not to destroy the Israelites, but rather for them to return to Him. He said, **"Come now, let us reason together"** (v. 18). The picture here is of the sinner sitting down and discussing face-to-face his or her situation with the living God. The Lord does not want mindless obedience, but He wants

His children to realize how harmful their sin actually is to them and to their relationship with Him.

God describes sins as **scarlet** (v. 18)—the color of blood. The Hebrew word for scarlet comes from a word that means to "double dip." The implication is that the stain is impossible to remove. Sin has caused God's children to be in a hopeless situation. Simply depending upon themselves was futile. Instead, God offered a complete remedy to cleanse them so their sins would be **white as snow** (v. 18), completely wiped out.

God is simply reinforcing the fact that His people—then and now—had (and have) a choice between a blessing or curse. We are given an option to either choose the way of repentance that leads to abundant and everlasting life (v. 19) or the way of our own sinful rebellion that leads to heartache and destruction in this life and the life to come (v. 20). The choice is ours. Which will you choose?

WORDS FROM WESLEY

Isaiah 1:19

If—If you are fully resolved to obey all my commands. *Shall eat*—Together with pardon, you shall receive temporal and worldly blessings. (ENOT)

DISCUSSION

The prophet Isaiah uncompromisingly preached God's message to Israel. What he told Israel is extremely relevant for us today.

1. How many reigns did Isaiah's ministry span? What is significant about such a long prophetic ministry? Explain.

2. In what sense was Israel dumber than an ox and donkey? How can a nation so blessed by the Lord become so dumb?

3. What words stand out to you in Isaiah 1:4–5 as highly descriptive of Israel's sinful condition?

4. What personal and national consequences of rebellion against God do you find in verse 8?

5. Do you ever feel like you are part of a small remnant of believers in a nation that has dishonored God? Why or why not?

6. What characteristics of God do you see in verses 18–20?

7. Why do you agree or disagree that no one's sin lies beyond God's willingness and power to forgive?

8. Do you think rebellion against God weakens a nation? Defend your answer.

PRAYER

Oh, God, show us our sin. Help us see how it offends You. Lay out before us the choice of blessing or curse. Make us willing to admit our sin so Your Son's blood can wash us white as snow.

2

ARE YOU READY TO SERVE?

Isaiah 6:1–13

God prepares us for His service.

A pastor was asked why his church was successful. "Well," he replied, "I preach every Sunday to about two thousand members, and then those two thousand preach throughout the week where they live and work."

The pastor and the church members understood that every believer is called to serve the Lord. They realized the truth that a church must evangelize or fossilize, send or end, be a missionary church or a missing church.

This study motivates us to serve as faithful stewards of the message we have received from the exalted King of heaven.

COMMENTARY

A number of traumatic events occurred within Isaiah's lifetime. One of these was the death of Uzziah. Uzziah started out as a good king, he was only sixteen years old when he was crowned (2 Chron. 26:1), and the exploits of his early years were amazing. He defeated the Philistines and other surrounding enemies who had been constant irritations to Israel (see 2 Chron. 26:6–8). Uzziah was a warrior, builder, gardener, farmer, and administrator (2 Chron. 26:8–15). Uzziah became powerful and full of the pride of his accomplishments. The one thing he wasn't was a priest. The kings of many surrounding countries, such as Assyria, were also the high priests of their national religions. Perhaps Uzziah, because of pride and power, thought he was being left out of this "kingly duty," so he forced his way to the altar in opposition to the priests who confronted him there (2 Chron. 26:16–21). He immediately became a leper, and for the rest of his life was confined to seclusion, while his son, Jotham, took active control of the kingdom.

Both Amos and Zechariah mentioned an earthquake during Uzziah's reign (Amos 1:1; Zech. 14:5). The historian Josephus said the earthquake occurred at the exact time when Uzziah made his way to the altar (*Antiquities of the Jews*: book IX, chapter X, paragraph 4). Josephus also seems to have viewed the destruction of the king's garden by a landslide as an additional punishment.

Uzziah's reign had brought a relative prosperity and peace to Judah and there was also, perhaps, a spillover to the northern kingdom. The prophet Amos, who was a contemporary of Isaiah, described the rich women of Israel as "cows of Bashan" (Amos 4:1), who oppressed the poor while lazing around drinking. Amos also described how one would know it was Israel that came to destruction by the items of luxury scattered in the debris (Amos 3:12). While Israel went through a whole succession of kings during Uzziah's fifty-two-year reign in Judah, they had also had success in disposing of enemies and lived in relative peace until the Assyrians began to invade. This was about the time Isaiah's ministry began.

Isaiah's ministry encompassed a time of great war and destruction, with kingdoms rising and falling in constant succession. Egypt, Babylon, the Hittites, and the Assyrians were in some kind of battle constantly. Kings and generals, like in Israel, were in constant power struggles with coups, coup attempts, and assassinations. In 722 B.C. the northern kingdom of Israel was destroyed by the Assyrians, never to rise again. The conquering king of Assyria (Shalmaneser IV) appears to have been immediately murdered and replaced by a general (Sargon). All through

Isaiah's lifetime, Assyria was a dominant force, constantly pressing Judah until the Assyrians were finally crushed by the Babylonians. The Assyrians were ruthless and known for their cruelty. The men of the nation seemed to have been primarily a standing army, and their primary national "industry" was war. The southern kingdom of Judah was invaded, but through God's intervention was saved (see Isa. 36–37).

This was the world in which Isaiah was called to minister—a world where warning was to be preached, but where destruction would eventually reign. Isaiah's job was to help Judah through the times in which they lived, to prepare Judah for a captivity to Babylon that was to come in a little over one hundred years, to preach the hope of return to the land following seventy years of captivity, and finally to offer the hope of a Messiah who would not arrive for over seven hundred years in the future, but who would definitely come. What a task! What a call! What a message!

When We See the Lord (Isa. 6:1–4)

One of the difficulties a prophet has in describing **the Lord** (v. 1) is that he has a limited pool of experience and vocabulary to call on in order to form the description. Remember that Isaiah was describing a scene that is totally outside physical experience, but he had to use physical experience to describe it. **Above him were seraphs, each with six wings** (v. 2). This is the only place in Scripture where this term is used to describe heavenly beings. In Isaiah 14:29 and other places, a similar term is used to mean fiery serpents. The root of the Hebrew word *seraph* means "burn" or "fiery." The wings are as confusing as the being itself. At least one set was functional: **with two they were flying** (v. 2). It has been suggested that the set on the face was to keep their faces veiled in the presence of God. The point is that these were amazing, powerful beings. At **the sound of their voices the doorposts and thresholds shook** (v. 4). They were in God's presence to minister to God. Their message was **Holy, holy, holy is the LORD Almighty** (v. 3).

WORDS FROM WESLEY
Isaiah 6:1

I saw—In a vision. *The Lord*—The Divine Majesty as He subsisteth in three persons. His train—His royal and judicial robe; for He is represented as a judge. (ENOT)

Throughout this passage and the book of Isaiah are glimpses of God's mission beyond Israel. Here it is expressed in the phrase **the whole earth is full of his glory** (v. 3). God's holiness and glory were never meant to be confined to one place or one people.

When We See Ourselves (Isa. 6:5–7)

When we see God, then we can really see ourselves. When we see real innocence, it reflects on us. When we see real beauty, it reflects on us; perhaps we would rather see ugly. When we see real holiness, it reflects on us.

When Isaiah saw God's holiness and glory, his reflection was **"Woe to me! . . . I am ruined!"** (v. 5). In this day and age, it doesn't take much holiness to reflect where a lack of holiness resides. Even a small candle is light in darkness.

The cure for **unclean lips** (v. 5) is a burning coal from the altar with which **he touched my mouth and said, "See, this has touched your lips; your guilt is taken away and your sin atoned for"** (v. 7). When the Holy Spirit reveals the truth of ourselves to us, He is always specific. Isaiah had a mouth problem, and that's what God's holiness reflected. When the Holy Spirit pinpoints a specific area of uncleanness, it can be specifically cleansed. That's how the Holy Spirit of God works. Satan, on the other hand, is an accuser: "You're no good. You can't live up to a holy life." There's no place to put the live coal. But when the Holy Spirit convicts, the place for the coal is evident. The cure for uncleanness is a coal right off the altar.

WORDS FROM WESLEY
Isaiah 6:5

I am—I am a great sinner, as many other ways, so particularly by my lips. I am an unclean branch of an unclean tree; besides my own uncleanness, I have both by my omissions and commissions involved myself in the guilt of their sins. *Have seen*—The sight of this glorious and holy God gives me cause to fear that he is come to judgment against me. (ENOT)

When We See Others (Isa. 6:8–10)

Once the holiness issue was taken care of, there was a service issue. **"Whom shall I send? And who will go for us?"** (v. 8). There is a dramatic picture in John when Jesus' disciples were afraid and Jesus appeared to them (John 20:19). He showed them His hands and side (v. 20) and then gave them the commission, "As the Father has sent me, I am sending you" (v. 21). Can you see that picture? "See, here is what it cost. Now, you get to go out as I did." In the next chapter, Peter said, "I think I'll go fishing." The command was not enough without Pentecost, and Jesus indicated that key in John 20:22: "Receive the Holy Spirit." When cleansing comes, then the answer to the call is **"Here am I. Send me!"** (Isa. 6:8).

Verses 9–13 is written in a poetic form. For Isaiah, his job is specific: **Go and tell this people** (v. 9). In verses 9–10, there is a kind of play on words and a repetition that probably sounds better in Hebrew than English. But the lesson is clear: This is not going to be an easy job.

Today, in evangelical missions around the world, we are seeing a remarkable revival. There are literally thousands coming into the kingdom every week. Churches are being planted at a rate that we could never have imagined several years ago. There is a place in Sierra Leone where missionaries labored for fifty years to see only two converts. The people were **ever hearing, but never understanding . . . ever seeing, but never perceiving** (v. 9). Surely you could say **the heart of this people** is **calloused** (v. 10). But today, we are seeing a tremendous harvest in that place, a harvest that could never have taken place without those who went ahead, laying the groundwork.

WORDS FROM WESLEY
Isaiah 6:9

Perceive not—The Hebrew words are imperative; yet they are not to be taken as a command what the people ought to do, but only as a prediction what they would do. The sense is, because you have so long heard my words, and seen my works, to no purpose, and have hardened your hearts, and will not learn nor reform, I will punish you in your own kind, your sin shall be your punishment. I will still continue my word and works to you, but will withdraw my Spirit, so that you shall be as unable, as now you are unwilling, to understand. (ENOT)

When We See Hope (Isa. 6:11–13)

Is it possible to see hope in its fullness without first seeing despair? Israel and Judah were going into a period of terrible devastation. At the time of Isaiah's vision, things were pretty good. There were enemies around, but in both Israel and Judah things were prosperous and peaceful. Major enemies from past decades were defeated and other bigger enemies were fighting each other and leaving the little folks alone. Verses 11–13 probably brought out the "crazy prophet" talk. "Did you hear what he predicted? **The cities lie ruined and without habitant . . . houses are left deserted and the fields ruined and ravaged . . . the LORD has sent everyone far away and the land is utterly forsaken** (vv. 11–12). Crazy prophet!" This was predicted in a period of peace and prosperity, yet it happened just as Isaiah said. First Israel and then Judah. Today, we look back and think surely they could see this coming. But they couldn't see any more than we can see where we will be in two hundred years.

But after the despair, there was a message of hope. **And though a tenth remains in the land, it will again be laid waste** (v. 13). But there will be a stump from which shoots will grow, **so the holy seed will be the stump in the land** (v. 13). Judah could not see the despair that was coming, but eventually they would see it and would then also envision the hope promised by the prophet.

WORDS FROM WESLEY

Isaiah 6:13

A tenth—A small remnant reserved, that number being put indefinitely. *Return*—Out of the Babylonish captivity, into their own land. *Eaten*—That remnant shall be devoured a second time, by the kings of Syria, and afterwards by the Romans. *Yet*—Yet there shall be another remnant, not such an one as that which came out of Babylon, but an holy seed, who shall afterwards look upon him whom they have pierced, and mourn over him. *When*—Who when their leaves are cast in winter, have a substance within themselves, a vital principle, which preserves life in the root of the tree, and in due time sends it forth into all the branches. *The support*—Of the land or people, which, were it not for the sake of these, should be finally rooted out. (ENOT)

DISCUSSION

Isaiah received a divine call to be God's prophet, but every believer is called too. We are ambassadors of Christ.

1. Why do you agree or disagree that the death of King Uzziah must have deeply disturbed Isaiah?

2. Has the death of a president or prime minister caused you emotional distress? If so, how did your faith in the Lord help you surmount that distress?

3. Why is it so important to remember that the King of Glory occupies a throne?

4. How does the heavenly scene described in Isaiah 6:1–4 affect your perception of God?

5. Isaiah confessed his sinfulness when he saw the Lord. Why do you agree or disagree that it is impossible to lead a holy life without holding a high view of God?

6. Do you believe unclean language is common among believers today? Why or why not?

7. Read 2 Corinthians 5:20. What calling have Christians received? What should we do if people refuse to listen to our message?

8. What hope do you see for our nation?

PRAYER

Heavenly Father, we see around us a culture so like Isaiah's world—sinful and increasing in sin—in danger of Your grave judgment. Please cleanse us, then send us to go and tell others how to find peace with You.

3

A FOREVER PROMISE

Isaiah 7:14; 9:6–7; 11:1–10

God promises a Savior.

A birth announcement typically includes the baby's full name, birth date and time, weight, and length. Sometimes it includes a photo of the baby. You can imagine the surprise recipients of one birth announcement experienced when a typo gave baby Christine's weight as 72 pounds instead of 7 pounds, 2 ounces.

However, Isaiah delivered history's most unusual birth announcement. The announcement came more than seven hundred years before the Baby was born. Furthermore, it declared that the Baby would be born of a virgin.

We know, of course, that Jesus was the subject of this unique birth announcement, but we learn more about this prophesied Baby in this inspiring study.

COMMENTARY

Isaiah 7–12 deals with the Assyrian threat to Israel and Judah. Judah was sandwiched between two superpowers—Assyria to the north and Egypt to the south. It was a foreign policy nightmare. Who could the kings of Judah trust? Isaiah encouraged them to trust God to protect His people from both these superpowers and every other enemy. However, they chose to buy peace from their enemies. God promised to judge them.

In spite of the godly heritage he inherited from his father, Jotham, and grandfather, Uzziah, King Ahaz of Judah (Isa. 7:1) "did not do what was right in the eyes of the LORD his God"

(2 Kings 16:2). He worshiped idols and practiced child sacrifice (16:3–4). Ahaz actively promoted wickedness in his nation (2 Chron. 28:19). As a result, the Lord allowed Judah's neighbors to attack and take control of large portions of his land.

Pekah of Israel and Rezin of Damascus formed an alliance and attacked Judah. They killed 120,000 men and carried away hundreds of thousands of captives. Then they laid siege to Jerusalem in an attempt to install their own king, but they were unable to take the city (2 Kings 16:5; 2 Chron. 28:5–8; Isa. 7:6). This was the background of Isaiah's prophecy calling Ahaz to trust in the Lord (Isa. 7:7–9).

In spite of these attacks, Ahaz refused to return to the Lord. Instead, he appealed to the Assyrians for help. Emptying the treasuries of the temple and palace, he sent all the money he could to Tiglath-Pileser III (2 Kings 16:7–8; 2 Chron. 28:21). The Assyrian king responded by capturing Damascus and killing Rezin (2 Kings 16:9). Nevertheless, this only brought Judah under greater Assyrian control.

Isaiah warned Ahaz that his reliance on Tiglath-Pileser was an insult to God, leading to his ruin (Isa. 7:10—8:22). Life under the Assyrians would be much worse than serving Pekah and Rezin (7:4). Instead of repenting, Ahaz formed an altar like one he found at Damascus and sacrificed to the gods of the Syrians (2 Chron. 28:22–25).

The Virgin's Child (Isa. 7:14)

Isaiah's appeal to Ahaz to trust in the Lord (7:7–9) is the foundation for this prophecy. After assuring the king that Pekah and Rezin would fail in their plans to conquer Judah, Isaiah told him, "If you do not stand firm in your faith, you will not stand at all" (7:9). Then the Lord invited Ahaz to ask for a confirming sign. God wanted the rebellious king to trust the promise. However, Ahaz refused to "put the LORD to the test." That sounds like a devout response, but it was a cover-up for the king's lack of faith. He had already made an alliance with Assyria (2 Kings 16:7–9). He would trust his worst enemy before he would trust God.

Isaiah responded, **Therefore** (since you refuse to obey and to believe) **the Lord himself will give you a sign: The virgin will be with child and will give birth to a son, and will call him Immanuel** (Isa. 7:14). This prophetic sign was given to Ahaz to guarantee God's promise to help Judah through their ordeal. It had a historical fulfillment. However, the New Testament gives this promise a messianic fulfillment. The Hebrew word for *virgin* means either a virgin or young woman of marriageable age. Isaiah's contemporaries could have understood it to be either. In reference to the Messiah, it unquestionably refers to the virgin Mary (Matt. 1:23; Luke 1:27). The gospel writers used the Greek word that only means "virgin."

WORDS FROM WESLEY

Isaiah 7:14

Therefore—Because you despise me, and the sign which I now offer to you, God of His own free grace will send you a more honourable messenger, and give you a nobler sign. *A sign*—Of your deliverance. But how was this birth, which was not to happen 'till many ages after, a sign of their deliverance from present danger? This promised birth supposed the preservation of that city, and nation, and tribe, in and of which the Messiah was to be born; and therefore there was no cause to fear that ruin which their enemies now threatened. *Immanuel*—God with us; God dwelling among us, in our nature, John 1:14. God and man meeting in one person, and being a mediator between God and men. For the design of these words is not so much to relate the name by which Christ should commonly be called, as to describe His nature and office. (ENOT)

The dual meanings of the Hebrew word were crucial for the prophecy to serve God's dual purpose of foretelling both the

Messiah's birth in the future and the immediate birth in the kingly line. A son to Isaiah's readers would have been an unidentified heir from Ahaz's house, perhaps his son Hezekiah. In reference to the Messiah, Jesus fulfilled it. Immanuel (God with us) was the name given to the child as a declaration of God's deliverance from the Syrian and Israelite coalition. In reference to the Messiah, it became a key name signifying Christ's incarnation.

The Sovereign Child (Isa. 9:6–7)

The king of Assyria who saved Ahaz from his enemies became God's tool of judgment (Isa. 7:17–20). When Tiglath-Pileser attacked, he came from the north through the lands assigned to the tribes of Zebulun and Naphtali. These people saw "only distress and darkness and fearful gloom" (8:22).

This dark gloom would not last forever. God "will honor Galilee" and the people will see "a great light" (Isa. 9:1–2). Everyone will rejoice in God's great victory (9:4). True peace and the removal of all weapons will come (9:5).

There is a surprise in this joyful dawn. A child's birth will usher in this age of peace, light, and joy. **For to us a child is born, to us a son is given** (v. 6). In contrast to the proud Assyrian king, God would deliver His people through a baby. This is an echo of the prophecy regarding the Messiah in the previous text (7:14). These blessings will arrive with the birth of the Son of God.

The government will be on this newborn's **shoulders** (v. 6). This Son will carry the full responsibilities of governing God's kingdom. He will be the sovereign King. A helpless infant will topple the oppressive enemies of God's people. **And he will be called Wonderful Counselor, Mighty God, Everlasting Father, Prince of Peace** (v. 6). These names for the Son set out an accurate description of His being and personality. He is Wonderful, a mighty work of God (Ps. 78:12). He is beyond all human comprehension and power. He is the Counselor, having no need of human advisors because He is divine. He is the Mighty God, King of heaven (Luke 22:69). He is the Everlasting Father, always protecting and providing for His children with tender loving care. He is the Prince of Peace, removing all hostilities and barriers between humans as well as between humanity and God.

WORDS FROM WESLEY

Isaiah 9:6

The' Almighty God is He,
Author of heavenly bliss,
The Father of eternity,
The glorious Prince of Peace!
Wider and wider still
He doth His sway extend,
With peace Divine His people fill,
And joys that never end:
His government shall grow,
From strength to strength proceed,
His righteousness the church o'erflow,
And all the earth o'erspread;
His presence shall increase
The happiness above,
The full, progressive happiness
Of everlasting love. (PW, vol. 9. 382)

Of the increase of his government and peace there will be no end (v. 7). In contrast to earthly kingdoms that grow through war, the Messiah's government will increase through peace. Moreover, His kingdom will keep on growing and never end.

He will reign on David's throne and over his kingdom, establishing and upholding it with justice and righteousness from that time on and forever (v. 7). The Messiah's sovereignty will be a continuation of David's throne and kingdom because He is "the Root and the Offspring of David" (Rev. 22:16). Justice and righteousness will be the foundation and building blocks of the Messiah's kingdom, instead of the tyranny and oppression of human empires. It will not end as the political and military realms established by humans. The Messiah will "reign . . . from that time on and forever."

All of this must be an act of God. Human babies are weak and helpless. Human adults cannot create eternal kingdoms of peace, justice, and righteousness. **The zeal of the LORD Almighty will accomplish this** (Isa. 9:7). God's zeal for His people and His desire to provide for and to protect them will make this Son appear in history. God will establish His kingdom with His birth.

The Spirit Empowered Child (Isa. 11:1–5)

Assyria was God's "ax" for cutting down Judah and the house of David (Isa. 10:5, 15–19). However, because of the Assyrian king's pride, the conquering empire would become like a denuded forest. "See, the Lord, the LORD Almighty, will lop off the boughs with great power. The lofty trees will be felled, the tall ones will be brought low. He will cut down the forest thickets with an ax" (10:33–34). The Assyrian forest will not return.

On the other hand, **a shoot will come up from the stump of Jesse; from his roots a Branch will bear fruit** (11:1). The glory days of kings David and Solomon will be forgotten and only the lowly patriarch Jesse will be remembered. In contrast to the Assyrian forest, this lone stump will send up a shoot and bear fruit again. This Branch is the predicted messianic child.

This shoot comes well-equipped. **The Spirit of the LORD will rest on him** (11:2). This is the Spirit who is the Lord. The Spirit will settle down and dwell on the Branch. The Spirit's presence in His life and ministry will not be temporary as it was in the Old Testament prophets and kings. The Spirit will reside on and work through Him.

The following three pairs of descriptions are not attributes of the Spirit. The Lord's Spirit is the source of these qualities in the Branch. The shoot from the stump of Jesse will have **wisdom** and **understanding** (v. 2) because the Spirit rests on Him. Wisdom is the ability to make the right decision at the right time in order to do the right thing. Understanding is insight and perception into the human heart.

The Branch will have **the Spirit of counsel and of power** (v. 2). As such, He will put His wisdom into practice by choosing the right means to make His decisions reality. He will also have the power to carry out His wise plans.

The Messiah will have **the Spirit of knowledge and of the fear of the LORD** (v. 2). He will know God, not simply about God. The fear of the Lord involves recognizing that God is holy and we all stand accountable to Him. The Branch **will delight in the fear of the LORD** (v. 3). He will display this attitude of responsibility and He will look for it in others.

He will not judge by what he sees with his eyes, or decide by what he hears with his ears (v. 3). The Lord's Spirit will guide the Messiah's decisions. His supernatural insight will enable Him to bring **righteousness** and **justice** to **the needy** and **the poor of the earth** (v. 4). He will be the champion of the ones ignored or oppressed by other kings.

The Branch is coming to engage in a very real struggle. **He will strike the earth with the rod of his mouth; with the breath of his lips he will slay the wicked** (v. 4). His spoken words are powerful and mighty. No one and nothing can prevent His victory over evil and injustice.

The Peacemaking Child (Isa. 11:6–10)

A little child will establish a kingdom that is completely free of hostility. Even the natural world will be transformed into a haven of harmony. **The wolf will** be the guest of **the lamb** and

the leopard will lie down with the goat, the calf and the lion and the yearling will dwell **together** in peace. **A little child will lead them** as a shepherd would escort his flock (v. 6).

This reversal of nature will extend to the ancient antagonism between humans and snakes. **The infant will play near the hole of the cobra, and the young child put his hand into the viper's nest** (v. 8). The weakest humans will be safe as they play near the homes of poisonous snakes. The little child will rule in perfect peace. **They will neither harm nor destroy on all my holy mountain** (v. 9). The Messiah will remove all aggression from the world.

His revolutionary peace comes when **the earth will be full of the knowledge of the LORD** (v. 9). All humans will know the Lord completely—**as the waters cover the sea. In that day the Root** (who is also the Branch) **of Jesse will stand as a banner for the peoples; the nations will rally to him, and his place of rest will be glorious** (vv. 9–10). Jesus claimed this two-pronged title at the close of Revelation (22:16). He is the Root (divine source), as well as the Branch (the human descendant), of David's dynasty.

WORDS FROM WESLEY

Isaiah 11:10

A root—A branch growing upon the root. *Ensign*—Shall grow up into a great tree, shall become an eminent ensign. *The people*—Which not only the Jews, but all nations, may discern, and to which they shall resort. *Rest*—His resting-place, His temple or church, the place of His presence and abode. *Glorious*—Shall be filled with greater glory than the Jewish tabernacle and temple were; only this glory shall be spiritual, consisting in the plentiful effusions of the gifts, and graces, of the Holy Spirit. (ENOT)

DISCUSSION

Centuries before Jesus the Messiah was born, God delivered the birth announcement to Israel. It served as a bright promise in a dark era.

1. What is your assessment of the spiritual condition of our national leaders?

2. Why do you agree or disagree that the spiritual condition of a nation's leaders affects that nation's peace and security?

3. Is the message of Isaiah 7:9 appropriate for our nation's leaders? Why or why not?

4. Compare the following Scripture passages: Genesis 3:15; Isaiah 7:14; Matthew 1:20–25; and Galatians 4:4–5. Why is the virgin birth of Jesus essential to our salvation?

5. How has Jesus been your Wonderful Counselor?

6. How has Jesus brought peace to your life?

7. Why do you agree or disagree that Isaiah 11:1–10 anticipates a future period when Jesus will rule the earth?

8. What differences do you see between worldly kingdoms and Jesus' kingdom?

PRAYER

God, we want to display in our every thoughts and deeds the fear of the Lord that Isaiah described. We want to know You personally. We want to honor You. And so, willingly, we place ourselves under Your authority.

4

GOD JUDGES UNRIGHTEOUSNESS

Isaiah 2:4; 21:1–10

Unrighteousness has been, is being, and will be judged.

James Holmes donned a gas mask and protective black combat gear when he bolted into an Aurora, Colorado, movie theater. Armed to the teeth, he launched tear gas into the crowd and then started shooting. Soon, ten people lay dead; scores were wounded; and several of the wounded were in critical condition. But James Holmes surrendered to police without offering any resistance, and then he told them he had booby-trapped his apartment.

During Holmes's first arraignment, he wore prison attire and was shackled. He appeared dazed and weak. The father of one of Holmes's victims looked at him and whispered, "You don't look like such a tough guy now!"

Isaiah described God's judgment on evil, bully nations. This study helps us see that even the vilest, most ruthless nations won't look so tough when God judges them.

COMMENTARY

One of the portraits of God painted in the prophecy of Isaiah is that of sovereign judge. We sometimes find it difficult to understand how a God of love can also be a God of judgment. Yet God's love and holiness demands that He judge unrighteousness. For without God's judgment of sin, there could be no true love or holiness.

The first twelve chapters of Isaiah have focused on Judah. We find the Lord through Isaiah rebuking their sin, prophesying of their judgment, and revealing the promise of future restoration. These chapters help us understand that God may use the ungodly to discipline His own people. Yet the deeds of the ungodly will not go unpunished.

Chapters 13–23 are judgments against the nations of the world. They are warnings to these nations of God's impending judgment. However, God does not judge without giving even the most wicked an opportunity to repent. Consequently, these prophecies are an invitation to the wicked to turn away from sin to the living God even though history tells us they did not repent.

Throughout these chapters, we see the severity of God's judgment on sin. Although we often try to excuse or explain away sin, our holy God does not excuse sin; He deals with it. That is why the Father sent Christ to earth—to deal with our sin once and for all. His holiness demands that sin be judged. Praise God for the sacrifice of Jesus Christ on the cross!

Instead of looking at the judgment for each nation, we will be focusing on only a small portion of this section—the judgment against Babylon. This is the second judgment against Babylon. The first one is recorded in Isaiah 13.

God Will Judge the Nations (Isa. 2:4)

The context of this verse places it in the future. It is speaking of the kingdom of the Messiah and paints a portrait of God as the one who will judge between the nations. God's judgment will bring total peace to the existence of humankind. He does not judge to hurt or harm. He judges to usher His perfect will into the lives of His people. Likewise, when God judges our sin, He then ushers His perfect peace into our hearts.

WORDS FROM WESLEY

Isaiah 2:4

He—Christ shall set up His authority among all nations, not only giving laws to them, but doing what no other can do, convincing their consciences, changing their hearts, and ordering their lives. *Rebuke*—By His word and Spirit, convincing the world of sin; and by His judgments upon His implacable enemies, which obstruct the propagation of the gospel. (ENOT)

Jesus taught about God's judgment of the nations in Matthew 25:31–46 in the parable of the sheep and goats. Note that both the sheep and goats represent the nations of the world. In this parable, God is separating the goat nations from the sheep nations. The goat nations are destined for the fire of hell, whereas the sheep nations are destined for His kingdom. We must realize that God not only judges the nations, but the people of those nations. We have a personal responsibility to live holy before God.

In Revelation 20:11–15, we see the final judgment of the unbeliever called the "great white throne judgment." Here the works of the unbeliever will be judged and punishment will be meted out to those whose names are not recorded in the Book of Life. Our works alone are insufficient to save us from God's wrath. We need the judgment of the cross or the blood of Christ applied to our lives.

However, we must also realize that believers will not escape God's judgment. We will not be judged for our sins because they were dealt with at the cross. Rather, our works as believers will be judged in order to determine our reward or loss of reward in heaven (2 Cor. 5:10; Rom. 14:10, 12; 2 Tim. 4:8). This judgment is sometimes called the bema judgment. Knowing we will not escape God's judgment can be a positive motivation for the believer to live for Christ to the fullest while on earth.

As we study this passage, may we be reminded that not only will the nations be judged, but all of humankind will be judged. We must take responsibility for our own lives. Each one of us must choose how we will live and what we will do with Jesus, our Savior.

Judgment Will Come to Babylon (Isa. 21:1–2)

This passage is **an oracle concerning the Desert by the Sea** (v. 1). **An oracle** is an utterance of God. The Hebrew word comes from the root meaning "to speak." Thus, an oracle is a spoken message of God. In this case, it is a word of judgment to the nation defined as **the Desert by the Sea**. This is a reference to the nation of Babylon, which was a desert empire just north of the Persian Gulf. This is the location of the modern-day nation of Iraq. Babylon was the capital of the Babylonian empire. In Scripture, Babylon can also represent all of the world empires that are opposed to the Lord (see Isa. 13:9–13).

In this verse, the prophet saw God's judgment as a gathering storm. He described it **like whirlwinds sweeping through the southland** (v. 1). This shows the severity of the impending judgment, since the worst storms came from out of the south (see Job 37:9). A storm in Scripture is a symbol of God's anger and wrath (see Jer. 23:19). God's wrath is compared to a severe storm in its impact. A storm in Scripture can be a picture of war as well. We can relate this to the severe hurricanes we have seen or heard about and the destruction that they leave behind. Storms gather and then leave devastation in their pathways (see Prov. 10:25). The judgment of God was about to come upon Babylon just like a severe storm.

The prophet saw a vision of **an invader** coming to overtake Babylon (Isa. 21:1). He called upon **Elam** and **Media** (v. 2). This was foretelling the events of the future when the Medes would join forces with the Elamites under King Cyrus in order to conquer

Babylon in 539 B.C. (see Dan. 5:31; 6:28). Isaiah would see this event through the eyes of the Spirit almost two hundred years before it actually took place.

WORDS FROM WESLEY
Isaiah 21:2

A vision—A vision or prophecy, containing dreadful calamities which were to fall upon Babylon. *The spoiler*—The Medes and Persians used treachery as well as force against Babylon. *Elam*—Persia, so called, because Elam was an eminent province of Persia, bordering upon the Medes. *Besiege*—Namely, Babylon, ver. 9. *The sighing*—The sighing and groaning of God's people, and other nations under the oppressions of that cruel empire. (ENOT)

Isaiah Reacted to God's Coming Judgment (Isa. 21:3–4)

Although Babylon was an enemy of God's people, the vision of this storm of judgment made a deep emotional impact upon the prophet Isaiah. He wrote, **my body is racked with pain, pangs seize me, like those of a woman in labor; I am staggered by what I hear** (v. 3). This was not the first time Isaiah was in deep distress over what the Lord had shown him (see Isa. 15:5; 16:9, 11). And he was not the only prophet who was troubled by the message God revealed. Daniel had a similar reaction (see Dan. 8:27; 10:16–17).

Isaiah's reaction was one of **fear** (Isa. 21:4). The judgment he wanted to see come upon his enemy is compared to **twilight**, which now has become a horror rather than a comfort to him. The use of the word **twilight** (v. 4) depicts the end of the empire. Isaiah realized how terrible God's judgment will be upon Babylon and the destruction that will result.

The word for *oracle* in verse 1 can also be translated "burden." Not only would the fulfillment of the prophecy become a burden to the nation for which the message was intended, but the prophecy became a burden to Isaiah as well. This tells us much about the man Isaiah, who truly knew God's heart and bore God's burden. As he saw in the Spirit Israel's enemy Babylon being judged, he did not gloat over their misfortune, but was moved both emotionally and physically by what he saw.

How often when we hear of trouble coming upon an enemy do we shudder with fear at what God is doing? Is that our first reaction, or do we feel a sense of satisfaction or even pleasure that they are getting their just due? Proverbs 24:17–18 tells us not to rejoice over the misfortune of others. This displeases God and may cause the Lord to turn His anger away from the one He is judging.

The Fall of Babylon (Isa. 21:5–10)

Isaiah also saw how totally off guard Babylon would be at the time of its destruction. **They set the tables, they spread the rugs, they eat, they drink!** (v. 5). In Daniel 5:1–4, we see that this was a picture of King Belshazzar's great banquet the night before Babylon fell. They were eating and drinking even from the sacred gold and silver goblets that Nebuchadnezzar, his father, had taken from the temple in Jerusalem.

The cry to **Get up, you officers, oil the shields!** (Isa. 21:5) shows how unprepared the troops would be to defend Babylon. The soldiers were commanded to oil the shields. The shields that the soldiers carried in Old Testament times were made of wood with a metal reinforcement in the center and covered with hides. If the hides were not oiled, they would become brittle and much easier to pierce with the sword in the time of battle. Thus, these soldiers were totally unprepared for the coming destruction.

WORDS FROM WESLEY

Isaiah 21:5

Prepare—Furnish it with meats and drinks. The prophet foretells what the Babylonians would be doing when their enemies were at their doors. *Watch*—To give us notice of any approaching danger, that in the meantime we may more securely indulge ourselves. *Princes*—Of Babylon: arise from the table and run to your arms. *Shield*—Prepare yourselves and your arms for the approaching battle. The shield is put for all their weapons of offence and defense. They used to anoint their shields with oil, to preserve and polish them, and to make them slippery. (ENOT)

How often are we ill-prepared to do battle in the spirit against our Enemy, Satan? In Ephesians 6:10–18, we are commanded to take the full armor of God and put it on. Just knowing that this spiritual armor is available is not sufficient; we must take and use it properly in our battle against the evil principalities and powers of our enemy.

The Lord instructed Isaiah to appoint a **lookout** (Isa. 21:6). The lookout, or watchman, would report **when he** saw **chariots with teams of horses, riders on donkeys or riders on camels** (v. 7). These riders would be bringing news of what was happening afar. The watchman was to be faithful to his task even though he may grow tired and weary keeping post (v. 8).

We too are commanded to keep watch. As a lookout of the Lord, we are not waiting for news to come of the destruction of our Enemy. Rather, we are to keep watch over our hearts (Prov. 4:23) so we will not enter into temptation (Matt. 26:41).

Finally, a man in a chariot relayed the news that **Babylon has fallen, has fallen!** (Isa. 21:9). The kingdom had been completely destroyed. In Revelation 14:8 and 18:2, we find the same message: "Fallen, fallen is Babylon the Great." Here Babylon represents the political and religious system of the last days under the control of Satan that is also destroyed completely. Once again God will ultimately protect His people and fulfill His purposes both in heaven and on earth.

DISCUSSION

The book of Isaiah proclaims grace, but also pronounces judgment—but it is God's righteous judgment.

1. Do you think modern-day nations are risking divine judgment? Why or why not?

2. Even nations that were home to the Reformation seem to be far from God today. How do you think this drifting away occurred? What lessons should other nations learn from this phenomenon?

3. Read Matthew 25:31–46. How does the nations' treatment of the Jews factor into the judgment of the nations?

4. According to Revelation 20:10–15, what determines a person's eternal destiny? Why can't anyone be saved by performing "good works"?

5. Why should Christians consider the bema judgment (2 Cor. 5:10) a strong motivator for faithful Christian service?

6. How does it encourage you to know that God is far more powerful than Babylon and all the nations of the world?

7. Should Christians try to persuade the government to adopt Christian values? Why or why not? If so, what are the best means of persuasion?

PRAYER

Almighty God, the prophecy You gave Isaiah of a far-off future reminds us of Your power, knowledge, and authority. We're grateful to be Your watchmen, and we ask You to equip us to take up Your armor.

5

THE RIGHTEOUS WAIT ON GOD

Isaiah 26:3–21

God brings peace through discipline.

A toddler was only inches away from a tiger, but he was safe. A video of the incident showed the tiger snarling and pawing at the little boy's face while the boy giggled and looked directly at his assailant's savage teeth. The more the tiger paced nervously and lurched at the toddler, the more fun the toddler seemed to derive from its antics.

Why was the toddler safe and unafraid? A thick glass separated him from the tiger's enclosure at a local zoo.

This study doesn't hide the fact that evil, powerful nations would like to devour God's people. The situation is no laughing matter, but God comes between volatile nations and us. While the world foments, all who trust in the Lord enjoy perfect peace.

COMMENTARY

The times in which Isaiah prophesied were quite tumultuous throughout the region of the Middle East. Assyria was the dominant world power, and Egypt and Babylon were power players on the world stage as well. In chapters 36–40, we read about one of the power struggles of that time. Isaiah 36 describes a siege of Jerusalem by Sennacherib of Assyria. Though the situation seemed hopeless on a human level, God miraculously delivered Hezekiah and Jerusalem from Sennacherib (ch. 37). Then envoys from Babylon visited Jerusalem to congratulate Hezekiah, and he received them warmly. God was not pleased, and later Isaiah warned Hezekiah that Babylon would destroy Jerusalem and take some of Hezekiah's descendents with him into exile (ch. 40). Nevertheless, in spite of the turmoil among the nations, God was still sovereign. Nothing would happen that He did not allow. Just as God removed the specific threat of Sennacherib, He was ultimately in control of all the nations, and God's will would be done. Isaiah prophesied this fact very clearly in chapters 13–27. In chapters 13–23, Isaiah described God's judgment against individual nations including Assyria, Egypt, and Babylon. Then in chapters 24–27, Isaiah focused on universal judgment and deliverance.

Scholars often describe Isaiah 26 as being part of a section (chs. 24–27) that some term *apocalyptic*. The entire section deals with God's sovereign intervention in history on behalf of the faithful remnant of His people, Israel. After pronouncements of judgment against the nations, chapter 26 opens with a triumphal song—"In the land of Judah: We have a strong city; God makes salvation its walls and ramparts. Open the gates that the righteous nation may enter, the nation that keeps faith" (26:1–2). Evil is going to be judged wherever it is found. Evil will be judged even if it is found among God's people. But the righteous will be sustained by God. A remnant of Judah will be faithful; that remnant will enter the strong city that God provides.

Chapter 25 tells of the disaster awaiting Moab. In this passage, Moab probably represents all the enemies of Judah and God. In contrast, as Moab is judged, the Lord Almighty will bless His people with a rich feast "on this mountain" (no doubt Mount Zion or Jerusalem). He will even swallow up death forever (25:6–12). The Lord has "been a refuge for the poor, a refuge for the needy in his distress, a shelter from the storm and a shade from the heat" (25:4). As Isaiah continued in chapter 26, he described the role Judah should play and the role God would play when He provided deliverance to His people.

Keep in Perfect Peace (Isa. 26:3–6)

Isaiah gave oracles of judgment on particular nations and on the entire earth in the preceding chapters. Though evil nations will be judged, those who trust in the Lord will not be disappointed. They will be in His care. Perfect peace will be theirs in the midst of trouble all around. **Trust in the Lord forever, for the Lord, the Lord, is the Rock eternal** (v. 4). The Lord (or Yahweh) is absolutely trustworthy and unmoving. Peace will reign for those who stay their minds on God and put their trust in Him even as the proud city is laid low. Through God's power, the course of events will be changed, and, instead of oppressing others, the proud city will be trampled by **the feet of the oppressed, the footsteps of the poor** (v. 6).

WORDS FROM WESLEY
Isaiah 26:5

On high—He speaks not so much of height of place, as of dignity and power, in which sense also He mentions the lofty city in the next clause. *Lofty city*—Which may be understood either of proud Babylon, or of all the strong and stately cities of God's enemies. (ENOT)

Way of the Righteous (Isa. 26:7–11)

What a contrast is drawn between those who follow the Lord and those who do not. The righteous have a level path; their way is smooth. They wait for God, who is the desire of their hearts. Judgments are sent upon the earth so that the people will learn righteousness (vv. 7–9).

However, **though grace is shown to the wicked, they do not learn righteousness; even in a land of uprightness they go on doing evil and regard not the majesty of the Lord** (v. 10). Why do people see the same events and yet interpret them differently? The righteous see God's judgments and learn righteousness. The wicked are showered with grace, but they do not learn righteousness. The wicked see uprightness and keep on doing evil, disregarding **the majesty of the LORD**. The perversion of the human heart is a frightening fact. Thank God for grace that moves us toward righteousness and regard for **the majesty of the LORD**. It is important to be sensitive to God's work on earth lest we become hardened against Him and His grace.

WORDS FROM WESLEY

Isaiah 26:9

In the night—When others are sleeping, my thoughts and desires are working towards God. *Early*—Betimes in the morning. *For*—And good reason it is that we should thus desire and seek thee in the way of thy judgments, because this is the very design of thy judgments, that men should thereby be awakened to learn and return to their duty; and this is a common effect, that those who have been careless in prosperity, are made wiser and better by afflictions. (ENOT)

O LORD, your hand is lifted high, but they do not see it. Let them see your zeal for your people and be put to shame; let the fire reserved for your enemies consume them (v. 11). God's hand is at work in the affairs of people. They did not recognize God at work. Do we? As God cares for His faithful people, His enemies will be consumed. We do not have to understand Isaiah or God as wanting the enemies to be destroyed. It is simply a fact—those who oppose God and disregard Him will eventually be destroyed, even though **grace is shown to the wicked** (v. 10). God made us free, and we must respond to His grace. What an awesome responsibility we have!

Lord, You Establish Peace for Us (Isa. 26:12–15)

In Isaiah's times and over centuries, God had cared for His covenant people Israel. The peace they experienced was His gift to them, not their own doing. As verse 3 promised, God gave peace to those who put their trust in Him. Isaiah recognized their complete dependence on God. It is always a temptation for God's people to trust in their own strength and ability, but God alone brings us peace. God alone works through us to accomplish good.

O LORD, our God, other lords besides you have ruled over us, but your name alone do we honor. They are now dead, they live no more; those departed spirits do not rise. You punished them and brought them to ruin; you wiped out all memory of them (vv. 13–14). How should **lords** be understood? Does it apply to human lords or pagan idols? Since **they are now dead**, it sounds as if Isaiah was referring to human enemies who had threatened or conquered Judah or Israel. Perhaps this was written after the siege of Sennacherib, but certainly there were others to whom it might apply as well. Isaiah 14:3–23 describes the ambition of the king of Babylon and his entrance into Sheol, the realm of the dead. This may be another allusion to the fact that every human power that had set itself up against God eventually failed. Death overtakes even the most powerful. Death is the great leveler. God is in control of history. Our only safety—our only peace—is in God alone. Soon the memory of those who now seem powerful will be **wiped out** (26:14).

WORDS FROM WESLEY

Isaiah 26:12

Willingly—Not from His own mere motion without a cause given Him from the persons afflicted. Hence judgment is called God's strange work. (ENOT)

In spite of threats from world powers, God has cared for and established His people. **You have enlarged the nation, O LORD; you have enlarged the nation. You have gained glory for**

yourself; you have extended all the borders of the land (v. 15). Judah's only safety and peace was in the Lord, and our only safety and peace is in the Lord. How wonderful that He invites us to be His children and heirs even as He accomplishes His will on the earth! If we trust in earthly powers, we are inviting disaster. God is our only security.

The Lord Disciplined Them (Isa. 26:16–18)

As the Jewish people trusted in themselves or in other powers besides the Lord, they simply experienced His discipline. Isaiah recorded the threat from Assyria. Back in the days of the judges, Israel had also experienced oppression from other nations. God disciplined His people whenever they failed to trust in Him alone. In their weakness and distress, **they could barely whisper a prayer** (v. 16). But God heard that barely whispered prayer.

Their accomplishments by their own strength were total failures. **As a woman with child and about to give birth writhes and cries out in her pain, so were we in your presence, O LORD. We were with child, we writhed in pain, but we gave birth to wind. We have not brought salvation to the earth; we have not given birth to people of the world** (vv. 17–18). On their own, Israel had failed miserably. God had planned for Israel to be "a light for the Gentiles" (42:6; 49:6), but they had failed in that purpose. They had **not brought salvation to the earth or given birth to the people of the world** (26:18). Considering all their failure, was there any hope? Yes, there was hope but only through the power of the Lord (see Isa. 26:12).

Dust Dwellers, Wake Up and Shout for Joy (Isa. 26:19–21)

Resurrection is not a prominent theme in the Old Testament. Verse 18 has sometimes been interpreted as one of the strongest affirmations of resurrection to be found in the entire Old Testament. In context, however, it seems to relate to hope for Israel that existed in spite of its failure to fulfill the Lord's purpose. They had been utter failures (see Isa. 26:16–18), but God could even raise the dead to accomplish His purposes. It may be a message similar to Ezekiel's dry bones that were restored to life (Ezek. 37). Whether affirmation of the resurrection of the body is the meaning or not, clearly Isaiah affirmed hope in spite of failure and death. Through the power of God, there will be life from the dead; there will be joy! We can have hope that God can take our feeble efforts and even our failures and turn them into life. What amazing grace!

WORDS FROM WESLEY
Isaiah 26:21

Cometh—Cometh down from heaven. *To punish*—All the enemies of God, and of His people. *Her slain*—The innocent blood which hath been spilled upon the earth shall be brought to light, and severely revenged upon the murderers. (ENOT)

Because of their sin and failure, God's people would endure punishment for a while, but God would raise the dead. **Go, my people, enter your rooms and shut the doors behind you; hide yourselves for a little while until his wrath has passed by. See, the LORD is coming out of his dwelling to punish the people of the earth for their sins. The earth will disclose the blood shed upon her; she will conceal her slain no longer** (Isa. 26:20–21). God's wrath would come on Judah for a while as later demonstrated in the Babylonian exile. But in His grace, God would restore them. Likewise, God will judge all who have slain the innocent. God cares for all people, and He will avenge the deaths of the innocent. Clearly, we have here a message for God's people Israel, but it also applies to all people everywhere.

DISCUSSION

Even in the most harrowing times, God gives perfect peace to those who trust in Him. Waiting on Him to accomplish His will is time well invested.

1. Have you seen or experienced a remarkable display of divine peace in the midst of stress? If so, describe the situation.

2. Find reasons in Isaiah 26:4–19 to believe it is always best to wait on the Lord?

3. What do you see as advantages of living in a so-called Christian nation?

4. What forms of discipline might God use to draw wayward believers back to himself?

5. Why do you agree or disagree that a Christian who fails to wait on the Lord might have to repent in haste?

6. What reason(s) do you think God had for not wiping Israel from the face of the earth when the nation became rebellious and worshiped idols?

7. When have you seen God's discipline tempered with grace and mercy in your life?

PRAYER

God, we need Your perfect peace. Keep us from focusing our minds on this world's many dangers. Keep us from trusting our ingenuity to get us through. Instead, may we always be focused and dependent on You.

6

THE WAY OF HOLINESS

Isaiah 35:1–10

God's way is holiness.

Colorado's most destructive wildfire—named the Waldo Canyon fire because it started in the Waldo Canyon just west of Colorado Springs—burned more than 18,000 acres, killed two people, destroyed 346 homes, and displaced 32,000 residents. It started June 23, 2012, and raged until firefighters completely contained it July 10. The heaviest toll of lost homes was felt in the Mountain Shadows neighborhood, where many residents returned after the fire to find only rubble and ashes where their homes had stood. Stately pines and grassy meadows that had surrounded their homes had become scorched and blackened. Nevertheless, many residents vowed to rebuild their homes and restore the land.

This study of Isaiah 35 anticipates a time when the Lord will restore the wilderness and other desolate places to Edenic beauty and peace. The ugliness of sin will be replaced by holiness. Our study offers steadfast hope and infuses joy into our souls.

COMMENTARY

The book of Isaiah falls into two distinct parts. Chapters 1–39 focus on God's judgment on Judah's distrust and disobedience. Chapters 40–66 focus on the hope of God's promise to deliver His people from both the coming judgment and its root cause—sin.

Isaiah 7–12 forms a section that deals with the Assyrian threat. Assyria, to the north, was one of the world powers at that time. Their kings sought to expand their empire throughout Mesopotamia. Egypt, to the south, was the other superpower. Judah's location between these rival empires put them in harm's way. It was a foreign policy nightmare from a human viewpoint. Whom could the kings of Judah trust? Siding with Assyria would provoke Egypt; while an alliance with Egypt would antagonize Assyria. Isaiah encouraged them to trust God to protect His people from all their enemies. However, Judah's kings chose to buy peace from their enemies. God promised to judge them for their lack of trust.

Isaiah 13–35 develops the idea that God is master of the nations. He will destroy the proud and violent nations and no one can thwart Him (14:26–27). The Lord will bring the Egyptians to their knees (19:12–17). Assyria will be shattered (30:31), and all who trust Egypt will fall with that nation (31:1–3).

Chapters 34–35 provide a figurative summary of this theme. If Judah chose to trust the nations, then the future would be like an ecological disaster area. If God's people chose to trust the Lord, then He would turn the world into a garden. Humans turned Eden into a desert, but God will turn the desert into a new Eden if we trust Him.

The Desert Blooms with Joy (Isa. 35:1–2)

Isaiah relished the use of contrasts. In the previous chapter, God's judgment on the nations turned their luxurious lands into a desert inhabited only by mournful animals. Now, he declared God's plan to turn a desert into a lush garden. **The desert and the parched land** (without springs of water) **will be glad** (v. 1). Commentators point out that in Hebrew the verb *rejoice* or *be glad* opens this verse. Isaiah emphasized the joy that comes when the Lord restores a devastated land.

The wilderness (between the Dead Sea and the Red Sea) **will rejoice and blossom** (v. 1). This whole chapter uses the image of a desert that **will burst into bloom** after a rain shower (v. 2). This radical change from death to life is a symbol for the life change God produces in those who trust Him. Just as the wilderness overflows with new life, believers **will rejoice greatly and shout for joy** (v. 2).

WORDS FROM WESLEY
Isaiah 35:1

The solitary place—Emanuel's land, or the seat of God's church and people, which formerly was despised like a wilderness, and which the rage of their enemies had brought to desolation, shall flourish exceedingly. (ENOT)

The glory of Lebanon (beautiful cedar forests and magnificent plant life) **will be given to it** (v. 2). This all is an act of God's grace—His generous love. **Carmel and Sharon** were also fertile areas known for lush trees and vegetation. The transformation of the wilderness will go beyond the simple revival of hidden life. The desert will thrive and become permanently green because of the Lord's touch. The desert, the parched land, and the wilderness **will see the glory of the Lord, the splendor of our God** (v. 2). All who trust in the Lord will enjoy glorious discoveries of God's power and goodness.

Encourage Each Other (Isa. 35:3–4)

Isaiah provided a practical application to this promising vision. God's people should comfort and encourage each other, especially those who are about to collapse in hopelessness and fear. **Strengthen the feeble hands** (v. 3) so they can grasp these blessings. **Steady the knees that give way** (v. 3) so they will endure and stand their ground. Encourage **those with fearful hearts** (v. 4, racing from fear) with the words God spoke to Joshua when he began to lead Israel into the Promised Land: "Have I not commanded you? Be strong and courageous. Do not be terrified; do not be discouraged, for the LORD your God will be with you wherever you go" (Josh. 1:9).

Your God, though He seems to have forsaken you, **will come** (Isa. 35:4) to abide with you. Immanuel, the Messiah, **will come with vengeance** and **with divine retribution** (v. 4). "But with righteousness he will judge the needy, with justice he will give decisions for the poor of the earth. He will strike the earth with the rod of his mouth; with the breath of his lips he will slay the wicked" (Isa. 11:4).

He will come to save you (35:4) from your sins. This is the root cause of all human problems. Adam and Eve turned Eden into a desert by trusting the serpent and rebelling against God. Judah's distrust and disobedience opened their land to devastating invasions. Immanuel will not only save God's people from their enemies, He will save them from their sins (Matt. 1:20–22).

WORDS FROM WESLEY

Isaiah 35:4

I nothing else require,
If Thou my Saviour be;
Salvation I desire,
Because it comes *with* Thee:
Thou, Lord, and Thou alone,
My whole salvation art,
Come, and erect Thy throne
Eternal in my heart. (PW, vol. 9. 406)

Healing and Abundance (Isa. 35:5–7)

When God comes, His touch will transform the lives of humans. Just as the desert will burst into bloom, **the eyes of the blind** will **be opened**, **the ears of the deaf** will be **unstopped**,

the lame will **leap like a deer, and the mute tongue** will **shout for joy** (vv. 5–6). God's presence in Immanuel will transform His people. Jesus healed the blind, deaf, lame, and mute (Matt. 11:2–6). He brought spiritual healing as well. Sinners will have the eyes and ears of their minds opened to see God's works and to hear and receive His Word.

Isaiah returned to the transformed desert image. This time the image is one of overflowing abundance. **Water will gush forth in the wilderness and streams in the desert. The burning sand will become a pool, the thirsty ground bubbling springs** (Isa. 35:6–7). In other words, the mirage will become a real lake. The most dry and barren places will be lush and fruitful. God's grace will flood the lives of the persons and nations who had been morally bankrupt. **In the haunts where jackals once lay, grass and reeds and papyrus** (which require moist soil) **will grow** (v. 7). Jesus said, "Whoever believes in me, as the Scripture has said, streams of living water will flow from within him" (John 7:37–39). John explained that the "living water" is the Holy Spirit that Jesus later gave to His followers.

Immanuel will radically transform the lives of those who trust God's promises. The apostle Paul compared it to the resurrection: "Because of his great love for us, God, who is rich in mercy, made us alive with Christ even when we were dead in transgressions — it is by grace you have been saved. And God raised us up with Christ and seated us with him in the heavenly realms in Christ Jesus" (Eph. 2:4–6). "When you were dead in your sins . . . God made you alive with Christ. He forgave us all our sins" (Col. 2:13).

The Highway of Holiness (Isa. 35:8–10)

Isaiah turned to another image. He described traveling to God's Holy City on a road Immanuel will provide. **And a highway will be there; it will be called the Way of Holiness** (v. 8). The highway and the Way are not two different ways. Isaiah used the parallelism common in Hebrew poetry to describe this road. It is a highway raised above the surrounding ground to make the trip easier. The valleys will be filled. The hills and other obstacles will be removed (40:1–4). **It will be called the Way of Holiness** (35:8) because the Lord intends for His people to share in His character. The people traveling on it will be righteous because of Immanuel's work in their lives. This highway is set apart for the persons mentioned above—the weak, blind, and lame—whom God will save. They are **the redeemed** (v. 9).

WORDS FROM WESLEY
Isaiah 35:7

Streams—The most dry and barren places shall be made moist and fruitful: which is principally meant of the plentiful effusion of God's grace upon such persons and nations, as had been wholly destitute of it. *Rushes*—Those dry and parched deserts, in which dragons have their abode, shall yield abundance of grass, and reeds, and rushes, which grow only in moist ground. (ENOT)

The unclean (who refuse to trust and obey the Lord) **will not journey on it** (v. 8). God will not allow it, and they will not desire it. This highway is sanctified and dedicated for the use of **those who walk in that Way** of trust and obedience. Christ will be the Leader on the Way, which is the reason it is also called "the way for the Lord" (40:3).

The phrase **wicked fools will not go about on it** (35:8) implies that this Way will be free of all who stubbornly refuse God's love and blessings. Psalm 14 describes these fools as those who live and act as though "there is no God. They are corrupt, their deeds are vile; there is no one who does good" (Ps. 14:1). These individuals cannot travel with Immanuel. The phrase can also mean, "Whoever walks the road, although a fool, shall not go astray"

(NKJV). The Way will be so plain and straight that even the simplest travelers cannot lose their way. The Holy One will walk in the Way with them. Jesus said, "I praise you, Father, Lord of heaven and earth, because you have hidden these things from the wise and learned, and revealed them to little children" (Matt. 11:25).

No lion will be there, nor will any ferocious beast get up on it; they will not be found there (Isa. 35:9). Wild animals often made travel through the wilderness dangerous. "The devil prowls around like a roaring lion looking for someone to devour" in the wilderness of this life (1 Pet. 5:8). The returning people will be protected against every danger (Isa. 11:6–9; Ezek. 34:25; Hos. 2:18). Jesus fulfilled this promise when He said, "I have told you these things, so that in me you may have peace. In this world you will have trouble. But take heart! I have overcome the world" (John 16:33).

Only the redeemed will walk there, and the ransomed of the LORD will return (Isa. 35:9–10). Literally and politically, these words apply to Israel's return from the Babylonian exile. Figuratively and spiritually, they refer to the redemption of all God's people—both Jews and Gentiles (Gal. 3:10–14). God's people, redeemed from slavery to man and sin, **will enter** God's Holy City **with singing; everlasting joy will crown their heads** (Isa. 35:10). Their faces will shine with joy and singing will fill their mouths (Eph. 5:18–20; Phil. 4:4). Their joy will flow from knowing that everything that could have prevented them from receiving God's blessings has been removed. Jesus said, "I tell you the truth, everyone who sins is a slave to sin. Now a slave has no permanent place in the family, but a son belongs to it forever. So if the Son sets you free, you will be free indeed" (John 8:34–36). The redeemed and the ransomed will celebrate their freedom as they travel with Immanuel.

Gladness and joy (not robbers or wild beasts) **will overtake them** (Isa. 35:10) to travel with them in the Way of Immanuel.

Sorrow and sighing will flee away (v. 10). "I saw the Holy City, the new Jerusalem, coming down out of heaven from God, prepared as a bride beautifully dressed for her husband. And I heard a loud voice from the throne saying, 'Now the dwelling of God is with men, and he will live with them. They will be his people, and God himself will be with them and be their God. He will wipe every tear from their eyes. There will be no more death or mourning or crying or pain, for the old order of things has passed away'" (Rev. 21:2–4).

WORDS FROM WESLEY

Isaiah 35:8

Holiness—The people (walking in it) shall be all righteous. *For those*—But this way shall be appropriated to those persons above-mentioned; the weak, and blind, and lame, whom God will lead and save. *Though fools*—The way shall be so plain and strait, that even the most foolish travelers cannot easily mistake it. (ENOT)

DISCUSSION

It is nearly impossible to turn hard, parched ground into a robust, beautiful flower garden, but God promises to do that and more.

1. What adjectives would you use to describe the wilderness after God restores it?

2. Why can believers look beyond the ugliness and gloom of current world conditions and rejoice?

3. Do you see a connection between human sin and blighted nature? If so, what? Do you see a connection between nature's future productivity and beauty and forgiveness? If so, what?

4. Read Isaiah 35:6–7. Why is water so vital to our planet's vitality? How has the water of life brought vitality to your soul?

5. How similar to Edenic conditions will our planet's conditions be when Immanuel restores it? Base your answer on Isaiah 35 and Genesis 2:1–20.

6. Have you ever traveled an extremely dangerous highway? If so, what emotions did you experience?

7. Why will it be such a safe, joyful experience to travel the Way of Holiness? (See Isa. 35:8–10.)

PRAYER

God, the psalmist prayed a perfect response, and we pray it with him: "Search me, O God, and know my heart. . . . See if there is any offensive way in me and lead me in the way ever-lasting" (Ps. 139:23–24).

FINISHING WELL

Isaiah 38:1–7; 39:1–8

God's blessings are to be used wisely.

The 2012 British Open ended dramatically and unexpectedly. With only four holes left to play, golf pro Adam Scott was four strokes ahead of Ernie Els, his closest competitor, but he bogied each of the holes. Ernie Els, on the other hand, finished strong and captured the winner's trophy and the 1.4 million dollar purse. Sports reporters called Adam Scott's miserable finish "the worst collapse in the history of golf."

Finishing well is not only essential to winning a sports competition, but also to gaining God's approval. This study examines significant chapters in King Hezekiah's life, especially the closing chapter, and it challenges us to finish well.

COMMENTARY

Chapters 36–39 are pivotal in Isaiah as a whole. These four narrative historical chapters are strategically placed between prior poetic prophecies of judgment upon the nations and the following poetic prophecies for the survivors of God's judgment. They are, on the one hand, a climactic description of the fulfillment of some of the prophecies of judgment. On the other hand, they explain, by way of introduction, why the following prophecies to a remnant of survivors will be needed. In this key section, the story of Hezekiah seems to flesh out and illustrate by example some key teachings of Isaiah about who God is, why He is completely trustworthy, and what happens when He is trusted.

It is likely that the chapter order of Isaiah 36–39 is topical and ideological rather than chronological. Chapters 36–37 go together and chapters 38–39 are held together by two linking elements in 39:1 — the phrase "at that time" and the reference to the messenger's mission to congratulate Hezekiah on his recovery. Scholars tell us that the events of Isaiah 38–39 probably happened before those of chapters 36–37.

But the time order of these chapters is not important to the overall purposes of Isaiah. Chapters 36–37 build upon previous material in the book and illustrate the trustworthiness of God. Chapters 36–38 illustrate how beneficial it is to trust God. Chapter 39 prepares for the next great event in Israel's history, the Babylonian conquest, the aftermath of which is reflected in the following chapters in the book. That's why Isaiah describes the events of chapters 36–39 in this order rather than in a strictly chronological one.

It is instructive to contrast the actions of Ahaz and Hezekiah in similar threatening situations. An interesting observation concerning this juxtaposition is that the place where the field commander stood to threaten Hezekiah (36:2) was the same place that Isaiah had stood to warn Ahaz many years before (7:3). Both kings were encouraged not to be afraid. But the lives and responses of the kings contrast sharply, and as a result, so do the prophet's messages. If Hezekiah is the positive example of trusting God, Ahaz is the negative foil.

Hezekiah reigned during the time when the rule of the ancient nation of Assyria was expanding. The Assyrian king Tiglath-Pileser (also called Pul) invaded northern Israel (simply called Israel) while Hezekiah's great-grandfather Uzziah (also called Azariah) was still alive. At that time, Tiglath-Pileser forced Israel to pay tribute (2 Kings 15:19–20).

God had warned Israel through Moses that He was going to execute His promised judgments against those who would not keep His covenant (Deut. 8:19–20; 29:22–28). Earlier prophets to the ten tribes of the northern kingdom, Hosea and Amos, had predicted destruction as a consequence of Israel's flagrant idol worship (Hos. 1:4; 8:1–6; 10:1–6; Amos 3:11–14; 5:1–6). But no one was listening. King after king continued to lead Israel in idol worship, following the example of Jeroboam I, who had placed golden calves at Bethel and Dan (1 Kings 12:28).

In 743 B.C. during the reign of Pekah, king of Israel, Assyria seized Gilead, Galilee, and the land of Naphtali (2 Kings 15:29) and deported the people. When Hezekiah's father, King Ahaz of Judah, had been attacked by King Rezin of Aram (Syria) and Pekah, Ahaz had appealed to Tiglath-Pileser for help and offered to be his vassal state (16:7–8). In reply, the new Assyrian king, Shalmaneser, conquered Syria (16:9; 18:9).

When Ahaz had been so afraid of Pekah and Rezin, Isaiah predicted precisely what God was going to do to punish Israel (Isa. 7:16). He also predicted that at the same time God would begin to punish the sins of Judah as well (7:20).

Assyria's main rival for power over Palestine and Syria was Egypt. The last king of Israel, Hoshea, quit paying tribute to Assyria and sent envoys to Egypt instead (2 Kings 17:3). In response, Tiglath-Pileser's son, Shalmaneser, invaded Israel and in 722 B.C. Samaria fell to the Assyrian invaders (17:6). The Assyrian tide did not stop there but flowed on into Judah.

Isaiah's earlier prophecies had clearly warned that Judah faced God's judgment too. The wickedness of previous kings of Judah who, like Ahaz and other kings in Israel, practiced idolatry would also bring upon Judah the curses of the old covenant.

The Assyrian strength continued to grow. But Hezekiah refused to serve Assyria (2 Kings 18:7), perhaps partly because he also was hoping for support from Egypt (Isa. 36:6). But when the newest Assyrian leader, Sennacherib, conquered much of Judea—including the city of Lachish about 701 B.C.—he also threatened

Hezekiah. Isaiah's earlier prophecies accurately depicted Hezekiah surrounded by the Assyrian host (8:6–8). This time of increasing national peril is the backdrop for Isaiah 36–39.

Hezekiah Responded to Illness (Isa. 38:1–7)

The wisdom of trusting in the one and only true God is illustrated again as Hezekiah trusted God concerning a personal problem, a life-threatening illness. The story is recorded in more detail in 2 Kings 20:1–11.

WORDS FROM WESLEY

Isaiah 38:5

Glory to God, whose gracious power
Is in His creature's weakness show'd,
Who turns aside the mortal hour,
And bids me live to praise my God!
To praise my God I only live;
To Him my residue of days,
His own continued gift, I give;
I only live my God to praise.
In love and pity to my soul,
Thou, Lord, hast snatch'd me from the grave,
Thy powerful touch hath made me whole;
O, who can as my Saviour save?
The Lord hath saved my soul from death;
Then let us sing my grateful songs,
And render with our latest breath
The praise that to my Lord belongs. (PW, vol. 2, 217–218)

The word from God through Isaiah about the finality of Hezekiah's illness might be troubling to us. How could this divine pronouncement be changed? Hezekiah responded to Isaiah's message with desperate prayer. His weeping shows his anticipatory grieving. He was honest with God about his feelings. The expression **wept bitterly** (Isa. 38:3) shows that he expressed his sorrow with some intensity. Hezekiah also described his emotional release in prayer in verse 14: "I cried like a swift or thrush, I moaned like a mourning dove." Sometimes in our prayers, we are afraid to let God know how we feel. How foolish of us. He knows anyway. How much better to be up front with our feelings in prayer as Hezekiah was.

If the king's description of his right living seems too good, remember that the writer of 2 Kings agreed with Hezekiah's assessment of his reign (2 Kings 18:5–8). While certainly all answered prayers are gracious gifts from God, nevertheless, the spiritual life of the petitioner is a factor. Consider the story of Cornelius (Acts 10:4), the advice of James (James 5:16), and the admonition of Jesus (Mark 9:29). Consider also that Isaiah would later point out bluntly that sin in our lives hinders prayer (Isa. 59:2). Most often, powerful prayers are the expression of sanctified hearts and lives.

What a wonderful comfort to us that God not only heard Hezekiah's prayer, but also saw his tears. This agrees with other great passages of similar comfort in Scripture (Gen. 16:13; Ps. 10:14; 34:18; Isa. 25:8). Apparently, the prayer of Hezekiah not only changed the length of his life, but also preserved his nation for many more years as well. The tide of Assyrian invaders flooded over most of Judah, having already conquered Syria and northern Israel on its way to also conquer Egypt. But by God's intervention on behalf of Hezekiah, Jerusalem remained independent.

Years before, in another historical contrast, King Ahaz refused to ask for a sign (Isa. 7). Hezekiah did not repeat that arrogance, but he did request what he considered to be the more difficult of the two possible signs suggested by Isaiah (2 Kings 20:9–11). God, who made all the laws of creation, apparently altered some for the sake of the sign as the shadow retreated rather than advanced as usual on the steps of Ahaz.

WORDS FROM WESLEY

Isaiah 38:5

Marvellously enough, Wesley's recovery immediately commenced, and he survived, from June 1775 to March 1791, a period of just fifteen years, and a few months over.

But even this was not all the wonder. Alexander Mather, at the time, was at Sheerness, in Kent, where he read, in the newspapers, that Wesley was actually dead. Mather says, he was not able to give credence to this; and, before he went to preach, he opened his Bible on the words, "Behold, I will add unto thy days fifteen years" (Isa. 38:5); and away he went to the chapel, and began to pray that the promise, made to Hezekiah, might be fulfilled in the case of Wesley. These are striking facts. We give them as we find them. The sceptic will sneer; but the Christian will exercise an unfaltering faith in the glorious text, which, in the history of the church, has been confirmed in instances without number: "The effectual fervent prayer of a righteous man availeth much." (JJW, vol. 3, 204)

Hezekiah Failed to Pray (Isa. 39:1–8)

Babylon was a rival for power to Assyria. So the visit of the officials from Babylon to Hezekiah was probably more than just a goodwill visit. It was likely also a diplomatic contact between two nations with a menacing mutual enemy—Assyria. It was a meeting of two potential allies. Perhaps this explains why Hezekiah was so glad to see them and why he bent over backward to show them such hospitality.

There is a stark contrast between the boastful monarch of chapter 39, showing off his riches, and the humble and repentant Hezekiah of Isaiah 37:1 and 38:2–3. Hezekiah, who had so often sought God in the past, did not seek Him here, a notable omission. He relied on his own wisdom. This reminds us that even someone who usually does well spiritually can easily have an unguarded moment when he or she does not act in faith. And such unguarded moments can have disastrous consequences. That is why we are warned, "Be self-controlled and alert. Your enemy the devil prowls around like a roaring lion looking for someone to devour" (1 Pet. 5:8). Hezekiah's experience reminds us to consistently ask God to direct our paths (Prov. 3:5–6).

God sent Isaiah to tell Hezekiah some sobering news. Had Hezekiah inquired of the Lord and found some of this out ahead of time, he would undoubtedly have proceeded differently. His own words condemned his ignorance when he answered the prophet's question regarding from where the visitors had come. God's prophet Moses had warned long before, "The LORD will bring a nation against you from *far away*, from the ends of the earth" (Deut. 28:49, emphasis added). In addition, God had repeatedly warned through Isaiah that He would bring down the proud (Isa. 13:11, 19; 14:11; 16:6; 23:9). The writer of 2 Chronicles said, "Hezekiah's heart was proud" (2 Chron. 32:25). We are reminded again that those who serve God notably among their peers are susceptible to spiritual pride. Now a humbling message came to Hezekiah: The riches he had proudly displayed would be carried off to Babylon and even some of his own children would be taken captive.

WORDS FROM WESLEY

Isaiah 39:6

The prophet having now foretold the Babylonish captivity, chap. 39:6, 7, does here arm his people against it by the consideration of their certain deliverance out of it, and their blessed condition after it, as in other things so especially in the coming of the Messiah, and the great and glorious privileges conferred upon God's church and people in his days. (ENOT, Isa. 40:1)

At first glance, Hezekiah's response might be interpreted as an honorable submission to the word from God. But the second part of his response evidences a selfish smugness. In contrast to his bitter tears when his own life was at stake, Hezekiah seemed relatively untroubled by what would happen to his beloved city and even to his own children. But before we condemn him too quickly, we have to confess how easy it is for us to downplay or even ignore the troubles of others if only our own circumstances are peaceful and comfortable. Looking at the wicked record of his son Manasseh, who succeeded him, perhaps Hezekiah could have used the words of Isaiah to prod himself to pay more attention to the spiritual training of the next generation. We observe that since Manasseh was twelve when he took office (2 Kings 21:1), he was born during those fifteen extra years God gave Hezekiah. Instead of enjoying his own comfort, Hezekiah could have been investing in the generation that would follow. Looking at it this way, Hezekiah sounds too much like many parents and grandparents today who pay more attention and invest much more money in their own comfort than they do in the Christian discipleship of the next generation. We should all pray, "Teach us to number our days aright, that we may gain a heart of wisdom" (Ps. 90:12).

WORDS FROM WESLEY

Isaiah 39:7

And of the princes—Here was fulfilled what the prophet Isaiah had foretold, Isa. 39:7. (ENOT, Isa. 1:3)

DISCUSSION

The apostle Paul testified in 2 Timothy 4:6–7 that he had finished well as the Lord's servant. King Hezekiah's spiritual life had its ups and downs, but in the end he earnestly sought the Lord.

1. God told Hezekiah to put his house in order because he would die soon. What do you think a Christian should do to put his or her house in order?

2. Do you think God would judge a nation if the believers in that nation disobeyed His Word? Why or why not?

3. The northern kingdom of Israel fell to the Assyrians mainly because it was steeped in idol worship. What kinds of idols do believers worship today? What are some consequences of this idol worship?

4. What is the best advice you could give your national leaders if the nation were surrounded by hostile nations armed with nuclear weapons? Defend your answer.

5. How do you account for the moral collapse of a prominent religious leader? How do you account for the victorious end of a life of service another religious leader attains?

6. What purpose did Hezekiah's illness serve? Do you think God uses illness sometimes to accomplish a similar purpose? Why or why not?

7. What advice about finishing well do you think is appropriate for a young pastor?

PRAYER

My Lord, we bow before You in submission. You know our needs and challenges. We ask You to work on our behalf. Keep us patient and dependent before You, so You receive any glory that comes from our lives.

GROW STRONG IN GOD

Isaiah 40:1–5, 25–31; 41:10

God renews our strength.

A lecturer on stress management held up a glass of water and asked the audience how much it weighed. After fielding some guesses, he said, "The weight doesn't matter as much as the length of time I hold it. If I hold it for an hour, my arm will begin to hurt. If I hold it for a day, please call an ambulance." He explained that the longer we carry our burdens, the heavier and more damaging they become.

This study encourages us to stop carrying our burdens. Our God is with us at all times, and He is strong enough to lift our burdens.

COMMENTARY

There is some controversy as to the authorship of Isaiah 40–66 as opposed to chapters 1–39. While there are some stylistic differences in the writing, style itself is not enough to bring this controversy when all the similarities are considered. The primary reason for the controversy is that while chapters 1–39 were definitely written within the time of the ministry of Isaiah, chapters 40–66 often project into a future time of captivity and restoration, which did not come for over a hundred years after the death of Isaiah. Of terms commonly used by Isaiah—such as "the Holy One of Israel," which is found thirty-one times in the Bible (twenty-eight uses by Isaiah)—about half appear in the first part of the book of Isaiah and half in the second part. The excellent poetic and lyrical forms of Isaiah's writings are found in the whole book. Stylistic changes could be attributed to age, the last part being written in Isaiah's old age, the prophetic vision being triggered by Hezekiah's foolishness in allowing the Babylonians to see his treasury (Isa. 39). John Wesley's writings in later years took on a different style than his earlier years, and yet we know for certain that he wrote both.

The controversy of authorship seems to come down to the issue of whether we believe God could reveal future events so realistically that even the names of deliverers not yet born (see "Cyrus" in Isa. 44:28; 45:1, 13). In the Dead Sea Scrolls, which included a complete scroll of Isaiah (the oldest known complete scroll of Scripture), there is no division between chapters 39 and 40. Keep in mind that the descriptions of Jesus the Servant (see especially Isa. 53) in the second part of Isaiah are just as clear as naming Cyrus. The Dead Sea Scroll of Isaiah is without controversy written before the coming of Christ. The only explanation can be the inspiration of the Holy Spirit.

Hezekiah made a big mistake. Isaiah 39 is the story of the envoys from Babylon that came to visit Hezekiah. Babylon was an old kingdom that was conquered and ruled by the Assyrians. Even under Assyrian rule, there was discontent and a series of rebellions. The envoys that came to Hezekiah were probably seeking allies to fight the Assyrians. Since Hezekiah had just experienced a scare and miraculous delivery from the Assyrians (see Isa. 36–37), he was probably not amenable to reengagement with the Assyrians. But he was friendly to the Babylonians and showed them around his palace, including the treasury. This really upset Isaiah (39:5–7), who told Hezekiah that everything in his palace would one day, but not in Hezekiah's lifetime, be carried off to Babylon. Hezekiah's reply was, "Hey, God is good. I'm cool, as long as it's not in my lifetime" (39:8, paraphrase). This sets the stage for the vision of the future that follows.

God Is Just (Isa. 40:1–2)

Justice is a term sometimes misunderstood because it means not only judgment and punishment when deserved, but also forgiveness and blessing when deserved. This passage begins with evidence of the imminence of God, the hand of God that reaches out to **Comfort, comfort** His **people** (v. 1). Some scholars believe this has reference to the devastation that was brought on the land by the invasion of Sennacherib of Assyria and the devastation brought to Judah, even though Jerusalem escaped total annihilation (see Isa. 37; 2 Kings 19:20–37; 2 Chron. 32:20–21). Others feel it projects into the future to the end of the Babylonian exile and the period of the return to Jerusalem under the leadership of men such as Ezra, Nehemiah, Haggai, and Zechariah.

In some ways, the time is not as important as the description of the nature of God contained in the passage. First, understand that God's justice demands that sin be punished; **her sin has been paid for, that she has received from the Lord's hand double for all her sins** (Isa. 40:2). Jerusalem is personified here, but the personification is a way of encompassing all the people it represents. This tells us about God. He will punish for sin, but will also restore and give a second chance if He chooses (for Samaria He didn't). God is just.

WORDS FROM WESLEY

Isaiah 40:2

Warfare—The time of her captivity, and misery. *Double*—Not twice as much as her sins deserved, but abundantly enough to answer God's design in this chastisement, which was to humble and reform them, and to warn others by their example. (ENOT)

The Lord Is God (Isa. 40:3–5)

For anyone who knows the New Testament, this passage cannot be extracted from passages like Matthew 3:1–3, which quotes and interprets this passage from Isaiah.

This prophecy is seen as being fulfilled in the life and message of John the Baptist, who was the forerunner of Christ. There are some important theological issues in the phrases **prepare the way for the LORD** and **a highway for our God** (Isa. 40:3), which are references to Jesus as interpreted by Matthew. These two terms are the most common names for God in the Old Testament. **LORD** is Jehovah or Yahweh, and **God** is Elohim. When Thomas declared to Jesus, "My Lord and my God!" in John 20:28, he was declaring faith in the deity of Christ and the removal of doubt. Matthew made the same point in Matthew 3. When we declare, "Jesus is Lord," we echo a refrain that has profound theological implication as well as personal commitment and faith.

WORDS FROM WESLEY

Isaiah 40:3

A second eminent sign of those times, the times of the coming of the Messiah, is given us in the third chapter of the prophecy of Malachi: "Behold, I send my messenger, and he shall prepare my way before me: And the Lord, whom ye seek, shall suddenly come to his temple" (v. 1). How manifestly was this fulfilled, first, by the coming of John the Baptist; and then by our blessed Lord himself "coming suddenly to his temple!" And what sign could be clearer to those that impartially considered the words of the prophet Isaiah (40:3): "The voice of him that crieth in the wilderness, Prepare ye the way of the Lord, make his paths straight?" (WJW, vol. 6, 305–306)

And the glory of the LORD will be revealed, and all mankind together will see it (Isa. 40:5). Another message, which was declared by Isaiah but not always understood, was the message of the mission of God to **all mankind together**. Jesus is the revealed glory of the Lord for all humankind. Simeon—the prophet who met Joseph, Mary, and Jesus on the day of Jesus' circumcision at the temple—understood this and quoted from this passage as well as Isaiah 42:6 (see Luke 2:30–32).

Jesus is indeed Lord for all humankind. He is the revealed glory of God. He alone is God's revealed salvation for all humankind. The Jews had a restricted understanding of God's mission that Isaiah, Simeon, and Jesus didn't share.

God Is God (Isa. 40:25–31)

While the passages above speak of God's imminence, this passage speaks of God's transcendence—the God who is God. God, who by voice spoke and created. **To whom will you compare me? . . . Look to the heavens: Who created all these?** (vv. 25–26). There is a whole series of rhetorical questions through this passage to which we must just stand with a bowed head and closed mouth. When God speaks, all we can do is listen and declare, "God is God! There is no one like Him!"

WORDS FROM WESLEY
Isaiah 40:27

What—Why dost thou give way to such jealousies concerning thy God, of whose infinite power and wisdom, and goodness, there are such evident demonstrations. *Is hid*—He takes no notice of my prayers and tears, and sufferings, but suffers mine enemies to abuse me at their pleasure. This complaint is uttered in the name of the people, being prophetically supposed to be in captivity. *Judgment*—My cause. God has neglected to plead my cause, and to give judgment for me against mine enemies. (ENOT)

So how could anyone say, **"My way is hidden from the LORD; my cause is disregarded by my God"** (v. 27)? There are a number of things to understand from this. First, God will know and see sin; God is just. Second, God will know and see a contrite heart; God is good. And third, God will know and see His children when they are hurt and oppressed; God is love.

The awesome power that makes God transcendent is the same power that makes His imminence so meaningful. Israel felt God's transcendence, while Judah was able to also experience His imminence. The nature of God was the same; the reaction to God's nature was not.

God is consistent: **The LORD is the everlasting God.... He will not grow tired or weary** (v. 28). God is compassionate: **He gives strength to the weary and increases the power of the weak** (v. 29). We don't have enough strength to always be on top of everything, old or young: **Even youths grow tired and weary, and young men stumble and fall** (v. 30). Some of life's trials may be our own fault, but some of life's trials are just life's trials. According to Isaiah, we don't have enough strength or wisdom for all of life's trials. Sometimes faith is touted as the elixir for every weakness, meaning that somehow "real" faith makes us super Christians. Faith *is* the answer, not faith in faith, but faith in the Lord, who can give you the strength you will need. Isaiah's message seems to be: "Believe me, you are going to need it." Faith doesn't mean you won't grow weary; it means the Lord will always see what you're going through and have enough power to share with you to get you through.

Here is the kicker: **Those who hope in the LORD will renew their strength. They will soar on wings like eagles, they will run and not grow weary, they will walk and not be faint** (v. 31). God can recharge your batteries. Judah was going through some tough times of recovery and renewal. They were going to face some things much worse, but there was **hope in the LORD** (v. 31).

God Is on Our Side (Isa. 41:10)

Perhaps we should say we are on God's side. Think of God's transcendence, this God who created all things by simply speaking. This God of awesome power and majesty says, **So do not fear, for I am with you . . . for I am your God** (v. 10). If God is as great and powerful, as we know He is, and He says, **Do not fear, for I am with you. . . . I will strengthen you and help you; I will uphold you with my righteous right hand** (v. 10), then we can say like a child, "God and I can do anything." God is on our side!

WORDS FROM WESLEY

Isaiah 41:10

Fear not, for I thy God am here,
(Jehovah to His servant saith),
My presence shall dispel thy fear,
And fill thy heart with strength of faith:
No longer troubled or dismay'd,
Perceive thy gracious Saviour nigh,
And every moment feel My aid,
And on Mine outstretch'd arm rely.
Why shouldst thou fear, when I am thine,
When all I am, I am for thee?
If thou art weak, My strength Divine
Is perfect in infirmity:
Without My help who canst not stand
Thee I will never leave alone,
But hold thee up by My right hand,
But lift thee to My heavenly throne. (PW, vol. 9, 410)

DISCUSSION

When we gain a solid understanding of who God is, our trust in Him grows stronger.

1. What is your opinion of the controversy surrounding the authorship of Isaiah 40–66? How does divine inspiration of "all Scripture" (2 Tim. 3:16) factor into this issue?

2. What characteristics of God do you find as you read Isaiah 40:1–5?

3. How does the shift in tone from judgment (chapters 1–39) to comfort (chapters 40–66) compare with the message of Romans 6:23?

4. How does Isaiah 40:3 affirm your belief in the deity of Jesus Christ?

5. Isaiah 40:25–28 reveals that God is incomparable. Based on this passage, what other words might you use to describe Him? Explain your choice of each word.

6. How has God strengthened you recently?

7. How does Isaiah 41:10 apply to any challenges you are currently facing?

PRAYER

Our Lord and God, we're both grateful and awed that You— almighty and holy—are on our side, offering forgiveness when we've sinned and comfort when we're crushed. Please equip us for whatever challenge we'll face today.

MOVING FORWARD

Isaiah 43:16–25

God is doing a new thing.

If you or someone else breaks a vase you deem valuable, don't despair. The Internet will tell you how to repair it yourself or contact a professional. If you choose to repair it yourself, you will learn that the first important step is to clean the broken pieces. Another important step is to purchase the proper adhesive. Further steps guide you through the restoration process.

This study points out that Israel needed to be restored to a proper relationship with God. The nation had failed to fulfill the purpose for which God had chosen it. Nevertheless, because God loved Israel and had good plans for the nation, He would cleanse it and bond it to himself. He still restores broken lives!

COMMENTARY

With chapter 40, a new section of the book of Isaiah begins. The previous study from Isaiah 40 proclaimed God's greatness and faithfulness. The message offered hope to all who place their trust in the Lord (40:29–31). Called the servant of the Lord, Israel is addressed and promised strength (41:8–10). Idol-making and idolatry are declared to be "less than nothing" (41:5–7, 21–24, 29). Isaiah's contrast between worthless idols and the Lord, who declares the future and directs the nations, is striking (41:25–28).

In chapter 42, Isaiah continued his description of the servant and his work: "I will put my Spirit on him and he will bring justice to the nations. He will not shout or cry out, or raise his voice in the streets. A bruised reed he will not break, and a smoldering wick he will not snuff out. In faithfulness he will bring forth justice; he will not falter or be discouraged till he establishes justice on earth" (42:1–4). Is this servant still Israel? Scholars recognize that sometimes Israel is addressed as the servant (see 42:18–25), but the description in 42:1–4 seems to refer to a servant whom God raised up as a replacement for Israel—because as a servant, Israel has failed. These new things portray deliverance from Babylon, but they seem to mean more, culminating in Isaiah 53. There the Suffering Servant is depicted in words that foretell the coming of Jesus, even describing His suffering and death.

Israel had failed, therefore, the Lord "handed Jacob over to become loot, and Israel to the plunderers" (42:24–25). Still the Lord did not forsake Israel. He promised to be with Israel throughout their troubles. Eventually, He would "say to the north, 'Give them up!' and to the south, 'Do not hold them back.' Bring my sons from afar and my daughters from the ends of the earth—everyone who is called by my name, whom I created for my glory, whom I formed and made" (43:6–7). The language seems to reach beyond Israel and her immediate troubles and out to encompass all whom the Lord will save. Surely this promise portrays the fulfillment in Jesus and proclaimed in the gospel. The promise is that sons and daughters from east and west and north and south will be gathered at the Lord's command (43:5–7).

Once again in 43:8–13 we see the contrast between the Lord and other gods. The Lord alone can foretell the future. The history of Israel had demonstrated the Lord was God, and Israel was witness to that fact. Verses 14 and 15 then set the stage for this study with a flurry of names and titles for the Lord. The Lord is the Holy One of Israel, and He judges sin. But the Lord is also their Redeemer who releases them from their sins. He created Israel when He called the Patriarchs. He remains their King, their ruler. In this study, Isaiah gave the words of the Lord that describe both His former actions for His people and His new plans for them also.

He Made a Way through the Sea (Isa. 43:16–17)

Before declaring the new things He would do, the Lord reminded Israel of the exodus, when He led them through the Red Sea. Not only did He lead them through the sea, but He **drew out the chariots and horses** of Pharaoh and **extinguished** them (v. 17). The Lord's acts in the history of Israel demonstrated His power and grace. The new message was to be seen against that historical background.

WORDS FROM WESLEY
Isaiah 43:18

Remember not—Tho' your former deliverance out of Egypt was glorious: yet in comparison of that inestimable mercy of sending the Messiah, all your former deliverances are scarce worthy of your remembrance and consideration. (ENOT)

He Did a New Thing (Isa. 43:19–21)

Israel's history was important, but they had dwelt on the past and God's care and covenant with them from long ago, neglecting the covenant in the present. Now the Lord was going to do something totally new for them. He was going to make **a way in the desert and streams in the wasteland** (v. 19). The symbolism shows that this new thing, this new way, would surpass anything the Lord had done for Israel in the past. Amazing! But they were blind and deaf witnesses to the past (43:8–13). Even the animals of the desert would honor the Lord for His provision of water. But the miracle of water in the desert was for His **chosen** people, who were **formed for** himself **that they may proclaim** His

praise (vv. 20–21). The mention of animals giving honor might be considered an allusion to the coming cosmic deliverance that will ultimately renew all things through Christ. Then all creation will honor and praise the Lord (45:23; see Phil. 2:10–11, where Paul applied this to Christ).

WORDS FROM WESLEY
Isaiah 43:19

A new thing—Such a work as was never yet done in the world. *Now*—The Scripture often speaks of things at a great distance of time, as if they were now at hand; to make us sensible of the inconsiderableness of time, and all temporal things, in comparison of God, and eternal things; upon which account it is said, that a thousand years are in God's sight but as one day. (ENOT)

What is this **new thing** (Isa. 43:19) the Lord will do? Surely it goes beyond the symbolic **way in the desert and streams in the wasteland** (v. 19). The promises continue building toward the revelation of the faithful, Suffering Servant of the Lord soon to be described in Isaiah 49–53. The Lord would supply a way for His people and water for their thirst, and that would be in ways that far exceed the future deliverance from Babylon (45:1–7) and the past deliverance from Egypt. The new provision would be spiritual deliverance and would meet their need for spiritual guidance and spiritual thirst. This water will **give drink to my people, my chosen, the people I formed for myself that they may proclaim my praise** (43:20–21). The Lord chose Israel and formed them for himself. In this "new thing," He would make provision for their spiritual transformation so that they would praise Him.

Israel Did Not Call upon God (Isa. 43:22–24)

Through the faithful Servant, the spiritual provision for the transformation would be completed. Verses 22–24 list seven things that either Israel or the Lord had not done:

1. Israel did not call upon the Lord. They neglected prayer.

2. The people did not weary themselves for Him. They did not have much time for worship and fellowship with the Lord.

3. Israel did not bring Him sheep for burnt offerings. Some scholars have interpreted this passage and other similar passages in the Prophets and Psalms as saying God was not pleased with Israel's sacrificial system. A better interpretation is that the people did not bring their sacrifices in sincerity.

WORDS FROM WESLEY

Isaiah 43:22

A new thing—Such a work as was never yet done in the world. *Now*—The Scripture often speaks of things at a great distance of time, as if they were now at hand; to make us sensible of the inconsiderableness of time, and all temporal things, in comparison of God, and eternal things; upon which account it is said, that a thousand years are in God's sight but as one day. (ENOT)

---

4. Israel did not honor Him with their sacrifices. Their sacrifices were formal ritual, not done from their hearts. Sacrifices were brought, but the people did not honor the Lord because of their attitudes.

5. The Lord did not burden them with grain offerings.

6. The Lord did not weary them with demands for incense. The sacrificial system was not designed to burden the people, but to provide for their spiritual needs.

7. The people neglected their offerings of **fragrant calamus** (v. 24) and were stingy in their sacrifices. Apparently, their hearts

were not devoted as they made their offerings and sacrifices, and the amounts presented were small.

With all these failures, Israel was certainly not proclaiming the Lord's praise (43:21). But in addition to the neglect in devotion and praise, **you have burdened me with your sins and wearied me with your offenses** (v. 24). Sin accompanied their failures in worship; perhaps we can even say sin was a result of their failures related to worship of the Lord. Is this not still true today? Neglect of our private and public worship often leads to outbroken sin in our lives.

WORDS FROM WESLEY
Isaiah 43:24

Sweet cane—This was used in the making of that precious ointment, Exod. 30:34, and for the incense, Exod. 30:7. Thou hast been . . . in my service, when thou hast spared for no cost in the service of thine idols. *Nor filled me*—Thou hast not multiplied thy thank-offerings and free-will offerings, tho' I have given thee sufficient occasion to do so. *But*—Thou hast made me to bear the load and burden of thy sins. (ENOT)

God Blots out Transgressions (Isa. 43:25)

Though Israel would be punished for its sins in the Babylonian exile, the Lord still loved His people and offered His gracious forgiveness. Through grace their transgressions would be blotted out, forgiven; their sins would be forgotten forever. In the atonement of Christ, God made the way for Israel and all humankind to be forgiven. It is both wonderful and amazing, the grace God offers to us in the sacrifice of Jesus on our behalf. That was still ahead for Israel at the time Isaiah proclaimed his prophecy. It would be a new thing for Israel, far more important than the past deliverance at the exodus. And later chapters in Isaiah make it clear that the blessings would extend not just to Israel but to all nations. We can understand these universal blessings to be bestowed on the church, the new Israel.

In 43:26–27, Isaiah invited Israel to a court setting to defend its innocence. However, the nation was guilty. The accusations went all the way back to their "first father"—who might be Jacob, Abraham, or even Adam. Then in chapter 44, Isaiah proclaimed promises of better days when their descendents would be true and devoted to the Lord. "But now listen, O Jacob, my servant, Israel, whom I have chosen. This is what the LORD says—he who made you, who formed you in the womb, and who will help you: Do not be afraid, O Jacob, my servant, Jeshurun, whom I have chosen. For I will pour water on the thirsty land, and streams on the dry ground; I will pour out my Spirit on your offspring, and my blessing on your descendents" (44:1–3). The "new thing" was coming. Jacob was even called "Jeshurun," which means "the upright one." Through the future outpouring of the Spirit, the Lord would fulfill His promises. Joel described the outpouring of the Spirit: "And afterward, I will pour out my Spirit on all people. Your sons and daughters will prophesy, your old men will dream dreams, your young men will see visions. Even on my servants, both men and women, I will pour out my Spirit in those days" (Joel 2:28–29). On the birthday of the church, when the Spirit came in His fullness (Acts 2), Peter used this passage as the text for his sermon. Indeed, we can understand these universal blessings to be through the church, the new Israel. Was Israel ready for the "new thing"? Are we open to changes that God may plan for us today?

DISCUSSION

Israel had failed the Lord, but the Lord would not fail Israel. He had good plans for His people.

1. What event in Israel's past conclusively demonstrated God's power and care?

2. What great things has the Lord done for you?

3. What principle do you find in Isaiah 43:18 that believers ought to apply? How might dwelling on the past hurt the future?

4. Read Isaiah 43:16–25 and then contrast God's good plans for Israel with Israel's actions. How do you explain the fact that believers may sin in spite of God's abundant goodness?

5. Read Isaiah 43:21. How well had the people of Israel fulfilled the purpose for which God had formed them?

6. Why do you agree or disagree that believers today are not fulfilling the purpose for which God saved us?

7. On a scale of zero to ten, which value do you think most Christians assign to prayer? Defend your answer.

PRAYER

Lord, in this passage, we see You as Forgiver, Redeemer, and Savior. We also see our imperfections—our sins. Please extend Your grace to cover our sins and make us upright, honoring You above all.

10

HE PAID THE PRICE

Isaiah 53:1–12

The Suffering Servant is God's plan for salvation.

Can you imagine how relieved and happy Barabbas was to gain freedom? He did not have to die on the cross that had been prepared him. An innocent person—Jesus—would die on that cross.

The name Barabbas means "the father's son" and adequately identifies every descendant of our first father, Adam. As such, we are sinners and deserve the penalty of our sins. However, another Father's Son, Jesus, died in our place. The innocent Son of God voluntarily shed His blood for us. As the Father's Suffering Servant, Jesus completed the mission for which He had come to earth. He cried out, "It is finished!"

This study directs our minds and hearts to Calvary and deepens our gratitude for our Savior.

COMMENTARY

God introduced His Suffering Servant in Isaiah 52:13–15. This Servant is the subject of chapter 53. The Lord began by saying, "See, my servant will act wisely; he will be raised and lifted up and highly exalted" (52:13). The phrase "lifted up and highly exalted" echoes Isaiah's description of the Lord in chapter 6 and elsewhere (Isa. 33:5; 57:15). The Servant has unparalleled position because He is God. As we read and study chapter 53, we need to remember that the Servant is the Lord. That means whatever happened to the Servant happened to Jesus Christ, our Lord.

This is an unusual man because He will act throughout His entire mission in a way that guarantees its complete success. He will accomplish all of God's purposes for His life. He will make no mistakes. The Servant will do everything according to God's plan to solve the problem of sin. He will experience true and complete prosperity.

Jesus described His own life this way: "The very work that the Father has given me to finish, and which I am doing, testifies that the Father has sent me" (John 5:36). "When you have lifted up the Son of Man, then you will know that I am the one I claim to be and that I do nothing on my own but speak just what the Father has taught me. The one who sent me is with me; he has not left me alone, for I always do what pleases him" (John 8:28–29).

In spite of His wisdom and success in fulfilling God's goals, the Servant will experience unparalleled suffering and humiliation. "His appearance was so disfigured beyond that of any man and his form marred beyond human likeness" (Isa. 52:14). This exalted one will be humiliated and maimed until He no longer seems human. His appearance will appall many and astonish the kings of the world. Nevertheless, He will "sprinkle many nations" (52:15) and purify them from their sins. His suffering will make forgiveness and cleansing from sin possible.

Christians have always associated this prophetic passage with Jesus. Philip used it to introduce an Ethiopian to Christ in Acts 8:26–40. Jesus himself may have used this passage when, "beginning with Moses and all the Prophets, he explained to [the disciples on the road to Emmaus] what was said in all the Scriptures concerning himself" (Luke 24:27).

Humanity's Reaction to God's Servant (Isa. 53:1–3)

Who has believed our message? (v. 1). We humans have a difficult time reconciling greatness with suffering. Like Job and his comforters, we expect evil things to rain down on evil persons.

If suffering comes into our lives, we ask what we did to deserve it. It is hard to imagine that one described in the same way as the Lord could suffer so horrendously.

WORDS FROM WESLEY

Isaiah 53:1

Who—Who, not only of the Gentiles, but even of the Jews, will believe the truth of what I say? And this premonition was highly necessary, both to caution the Jews that they should not stumble at this stone, and to instruct the Gentiles that they should not be seduced with their example. *The arm*—The Messiah, called the arm or power of God, because the almighty power of God was seated in Him. *Revealed*—Inwardly and with power. (ENOT)

The Servant **grew up** in the Lord's sight **like a** precious, **tender shoot, and like a** rare **root** springing to life **out of dry ground** (v. 2). But to the powerful leaders of this world, He appeared to have **no beauty or majesty to attract us to him, nothing in his appearance that we should desire him** (v. 2). He appeared to be an average person. He did not stand head and shoulders over others like King Saul. He did not conquer giants like David. He did not collect large amounts of gold and fine clothes like Solomon. God's Servant did not seem to be "highly exalted" to those who met Him on the street. One of Jesus' disciples asked, "Can anything good come out of Nazareth?" (John 1:46).

However, humanity's reaction to God's Servant went beyond ignoring Him. **He was despised and rejected by men** (Isa. 53:3). Religious and political leaders conspired to kill Jesus (Matt. 12:14; 26:4). And Jesus' disciples betrayed, denied, and deserted Him (Matt. 26:47–56, 69–75). **He was . . . a man of sorrows** (physical and mental illnesses)**, and familiar with suffering** (Isa. 53:3). Sickness and suffering are often associated with judgment against sin. Many people assume that anyone experiencing sorrows and suffering is an evil person. This attitude is revealed by Job and his comforters. **Like one from whom men hide their faces** the Servant **was despised, and we esteemed him not** (v. 3). In other words, we thought He was nothing more than an isolated fanatic who deserved what happened to Him.

The Servant's Suffering for Us (Isa. 53:4–6)

The word **surely** (v. 4) focuses our attention on the true reason for the Servant's suffering. This passage emphasizes the contrast between God's Servant and us. He **took up our infirmities and carried** (picked up and took away) **our sorrows** (v. 4). Everything we thought He had coming to Him was in reality our sickness and sorrow. Matthew stated that Jesus fulfilled this prophecy by healing the sick and casting out demons (8:16–17). **Yet** (in contrast to reality) **we considered him stricken by God, smitten by him, and afflicted** (Isa. 53:4).

WORDS FROM WESLEY

Isaiah 53:5

Pardon through Thy wounds I have:
But is pardon all the cure?
Thou wilt to the utmost save,
Make mine inmost nature pure,
Me to perfect health restore:
Then I shall relapse no more. (PW, vol. 9, 439)

We assumed God was punishing the Servant for His own sins, **but he was pierced** (bored through) **for our transgressions** (our rebellious acts); **he was crushed** (shattered) **for our iniquities** (our perverted crookedness and bent to sin); **the punishment** (chastisement and discipline) **that brought us peace was upon**

him (v. 5). The Hebrew word for peace means far more than the mere absence of conflict. *Shalom* implies everything humans need for well being. **By his wounds we are healed** (v. 5). Healing for all of our infirmities and sorrows is available because the Servant was punished in our place. Every area of our lives and existence is touched by the Servant's sacrifice.

We all . . . us all (v. 6)—these two phrases indicate the universal problem of sin and the universal solution of the Servant's sacrifice. **We all, like sheep, have gone astray** (v. 6). Every human being, in all times and in all places, has wandered off course into trouble. **Each of us has turned to his own way** (v. 6). All the sons and daughters of Adam and Eve have transferred their allegiance to self and "although they knew God, they neither glorified him as God nor gave thanks to him" (Rom. 1:21). **And the LORD has laid on him the iniquity of us all** (Isa. 53:6). The guilt and weight of every sin was His burden to carry because the Lord laid it on His back.

WORDS FROM WESLEY
Isaiah 53:6

We—All mankind. *Astray*—From God. *Have turned*—In general, to the way of sin, which may well be called a man's own way, because sin is natural to us, inherent in us, born with us; and in particular, to those several paths, which several men chuse, according to their different opinions, and circumstances. *Hath laid*—Heb. hath made to meet, as all the rivers meet in the sea. *The iniquity*—Not properly, for he knew no sin; but the punishment of iniquity, as that word is frequently used. That which was due for all the sins of all mankind, which must needs be so heavy a load, that if he had not been God as well as man, he must have sunk under the burden. (ENOT)

The Servant's Death and Burial (Isa. 53:7–9)

He was oppressed (harshly treated) **and afflicted, yet he did not open his mouth; he was led like a lamb to the slaughter** (or sacrifice)**, and as a sheep before her shearers is silent, so he did not open his mouth** (v. 7). This silence is based on two things. First, there is no real need to answer false charges. The Servant was innocent of any crime (Luke 23:4). Second, there is no real defense against charges brought in a false court. The trials were a pretense intended to cover up the plan to kill the Servant. **By oppression and judgment he was taken away** (Isa. 53:8). The Servant was the victim of a judicial crime and tyranny. He was executed because of an oppressive judgment leveled against Him. But all this happened to Him because He willingly submitted to it.

And who can speak of his descendants (v. 8)? His continuing influence in this world ended with His death; He had no natural children in spite of some popular theories. **For he was cut off from the land of the living** (v. 8). But the reason for His untimely death was **the transgression of my people** (v. 8).

Verse 9 contains a prophecy of a minor detail unassociated with the Servant's mission, but it proves which unjust execution was meant. The Servant **was assigned a grave with the wicked** (v. 9). Jesus was crucified between two thieves and would have been buried with them. However, the Servant ended up being buried **with the rich in his death** (v. 9). Jesus was interred in the tomb of Joseph of Arimathea, who was a rich and influential man.

The Servant's illegal torture and death happened even **though he had done no violence, nor was any deceit in his mouth** (v. 9). Isaiah emphasized the substitutionary death of the Servant throughout this passage. The Servant died, was innocent of all sin, but He died for all our sins.

God's Plan for His Servant (Isa. 53:10–12)

Even though the Servant was completely innocent, **it was the LORD's will to crush him and cause him to suffer** (v. 10; see also Gen. 3:15). The oppressive judgment, abuse, and execution of the Servant were part of God's plan for Him. Before creation and the fall of Adam, the Lord had decided His Servant would be a Lamb of sacrifice (Rev. 13:8). He had even determined that all who believed in the Servant would be His chosen ones (John 3:16–21; Eph. 1:1–14). The Lord determined to use this act of injustice to justify us (Rom. 3:25–26).

And though the LORD makes his life a guilt offering, he will see his offspring (Isa. 53:10). Here is the answer to the question raised in verse 8, "And who can speak of his descendants?" As a result of giving himself as a sacrifice, the Servant, who was killed in His prime with no hope of continuing influence, will see generation after generation come into His family. This is the first of three prophecies pointing toward the resurrection of the Servant. If He remained dead, He would not see anything. He must be raised to life again in order to see his offspring.

The second prophecy of the resurrection is also in this verse. **The LORD . . . will . . . prolong his days, and the will of the LORD will prosper in his hand** (v. 10). The only way the Servant can **prolong his days** following His death is to be resurrected. Again, **the will of the LORD** cannot prosper in the hand of a corpse. The Servant will rise from His grave and continue the work God planned for Him to do.

The third prophecy is straightforward and clear for all to see. **After the suffering of his soul, he will see the light of life and be satisfied** (v. 11). The Servant will conquer death. He will rise from His grave and **see the light of life**.

By his knowledge my righteous servant will justify many, and he will bear their iniquities (v. 11). Many will be counted righteous because they know the Servant. He will carry their sins and they will receive His righteousness. God considers all who receive the Servant guilt-free because of His sacrifice.

WORDS FROM WESLEY

Isaiah 53:11

Shall see — He shall enjoy. *The travel* — The blessed fruit of all His labours, and sufferings. *Satisfied* — He shall esteem His own and His Father's glory, and the salvation of His people, an abundant recompence. *By his knowledge* — By the knowledge of Him. *Justify* — Acquit them from the guilt of their sins, and all the dreadful consequences thereof. And Christ is said to justify sinners meritoriously, because He purchases and procures it for us. *Many* — An innumerable company of all nations. *For* — For He shall satisfy the justice of God, by bearing the punishment due to their sins. (ENOT)

The Lord's promise concludes this great chapter. **Therefore** (because My Servant has done all that I asked of Him) **I will give him a portion among the great, and he will divide the spoils with the strong** (v. 12). God guarantees that His Servant will be known as a conquering hero. The reason for the Lord's favor is repeated — **because he poured out his life unto death, and was numbered with the transgressors. For he bore the sin of many, and made** (or will make) **intercession for the transgressors** (v. 12). Intercession is the Servant's unfinished ministry. The language indicates that it is a repeated action with no stopping point. He will keep on interceding for us. The Bible assures us that Jesus lives to intercede for us (Rom. 8:34; Heb. 7:25).

DISCUSSION

Jesus paid the price of our redemption, not with His sinless life, but with His shed blood.

1. Why is "my servant" (Isa. 52:13) an appropriate designation for Jesus Christ?

2. How does Mark 10:45 compare with the prophecy of Isaiah 52:13 and 53:1–7?

3. Do you think artists' illustrations of Jesus on the cross accurately portray Him? Why or why not?

4. Why did Jesus' own people reject Him? Why do so many people reject Him now?

5. Although Jesus died to save us, why was it essential that He led a sinless life? (See 2 Cor. 5:21 and 1 Pet. 1:18–19.)

6. What do you think is the best way to express your gratitude for what Jesus did for you on the cross? (See 2 Cor. 6:19–20.)

PRAYER

Dearest Lord, this picture of the suffering You endured in our place makes us shudder. We could never have withstood the torture our sin required. Although it seems insufficient, we offer You all we have: our awe, gratitude, and worship.

11

COME, ALL WHO ARE THIRSTY

Isaiah 55:1–13

God's gracious invitation deserves a sincere response.

How long can a human being survive without water? About one or two weeks seems to be the average survival time, but who would purposely forego water for that long? If you were trapped in rubble caused by a tornado or an earthquake, you might not have a choice, and your thirst would be enormous as days without water increased. Most of us long for a drink of water after spending only minutes under the hot sun, so we reach for water as soon as we can.

Human beings also long for whatever we think will satisfy our thirsty souls. Some reach for fun, prosperity, or social relationships. However, as this study shows, only God can satisfy spiritual thirst, and He offers to quench that thirst free of charge. You will want to invite spiritually thirsty people to accept His gracious offer.

COMMENTARY

We see references to salvation throughout the Old Testament. Many are in regard to everyday types of deliverance, such as from disease, enemies, and physical threats. There are also those major deliverances that are specifically interpreted as being part of God's matchless and singular concern in human history as well as special revelations of His character and will.

In the New Testament, Jesus is portrayed as the Savior of sinners. The title reserved for God in the Old Testament is transferred to Jesus as Incarnate Son. He is the Savior and Deliverer from sin and its consequences, as well as from Satan and his power.

In this great prophetic section of Scripture, Isaiah opened with an invitation—"Come, all you who are thirsty" (55:1). Not only the Jews, though they heard the word of salvation first, but also the Gentiles, the poor, the blind, and the disfigured are called to this marriage supper, all who can be picked up out of the highways and the hedges.

The Israelites were being called to return and be restored. The whole book of Isaiah is built around the full extremes of God's judgment and salvation. He warned of wrath and punishment (42:25). In spite of their repeated disobedience in Isaiah 14:1–2, God showed compassion and promised to rescue them from oppression. This time of restoration redeemed them (41:14), saved them (49:8), and led them home (45:13).

God's Word never returns empty and will accomplish His desires (55:11). In verses 11–15, there is great contrast between what has been and what will be. Sorrow is replaced by joy (55:12). The desolation of the wilderness is replaced by the very elements He created giving praise to their Creator. The thorns and briers replaced by pines and myrtles (55:13) is another reminder that the land will receive restoration, too.

Only a God who is "I Am" could lay out the plan of salvation so clearly. The invitation is extended and is available to all who thirst, are willing to listen, and want to accept the gift that is freely offered.

An Invitation to Whom (Isa. 55:1–5)?

What is the first qualification required in those who are invited? They must thirst (v. 1). Everyone will be welcome to receive the gospel of grace under those terms. Those who are satisfied with the world and its pleasures and look for happiness in themselves, instead of seeking the favor of God, will depend upon the merit of their own works for righteousness. These people see no need to have Christ and His righteousness. They do not thirst; they have no sense of their need or uneasiness about their souls. But those who thirst are invited to the waters, as those who labor and are heavy-laden are invited to Christ for rest. Where God gives grace, He first causes us to have a thirsting for it; and where He has given a thirsting for it, He will satisfy the thirst.

WORDS FROM WESLEY

Isaiah 55:1

Come all the lost race, redeem'd from your fall;
A fountain of grace is open'd for all:
Your God's invitation discovers the stream;
The wells of salvation are open'd in Him.
Who seek to be bless'd, but labour in vain,
And sigh for the rest ye cannot attain,
Come all to the Saviour, your life-giving Lord,
And find in His favour your Eden restored.
Poor vagabonds here who shadows pursue,
To Jesus draw near for happiness true.
Ye all may receive it (good news for the poor),
And when ye believe it, your pardon is sure.
Come, taste, and confess the goodness Divine,
The sense of His grace is better than wine:
'Tis sweeter than honey, the milk of the word;
'Tis bought without money, the love of your Lord.
No goodness have ye, no goodness ye need;
His mercy is free, is mercy indeed!
Renounce your own merit, and buy without price
His grace and His Spirit, and crown in the skies.
(PW, vol. 9, 444–445)

There is free communication in this provision: **Buy wine and milk without money, and without cost** (v. 1). This seems to be a strange way of buying, not only without ready money, but without any money or the promise of any. We will benefit from the goodness of grace, though we are unworthy of it and cannot understand how something of such worth can be given at no cost to us. If Christ and heaven are God's gift to us, we need to see ourselves forever indebted to free grace.

What is it that God proposes? **Why spend . . . your labor on what does not satisfy** (v. 2)? The New Testament echoes this in Revelation 3:17–19: "You say I am rich. . . . But you do not realize that you are wretched, pitiful, poor, blind and naked . . . buy from me gold refined in the fire. . . . If anyone hears my voice and opens the door." The arrogance of the things of this world can be difficult. They are not bread, not proper food for a soul; they don't give adequate nourishment. Bread is the stuff of life but gives no support to the spiritual life. All the wealth and pleasure in the world will not make one meal for a soul. **Listen, listen to me** (Isa. 55:2). Not only listen to Me, but agree with what I say and apply it to yourselves. "Incline your ear" (v. 3 KJV) just like you do when you show concern; bend your ear this way, that you may hear and give answer; hear, **and come to me** (v. 3). Not only come and meet with God, but comply with His terms; accept God's offers as beneficial and answer His demands as sound. The invitation repeats itself—come all who thirst, come to the waters, come buy—there is urgency, a command for action. In verse 3, there is also the reminder of God's covenant with David. The relationship is not superficial, not like the world, but holy. **Hear me that your soul may live. I will make an everlasting covenant with you, my faithful love promised to David** (v. 3; see Ps. 89:28–29). God promised to put himself into covenant relationship with you and thereby place upon you the covenant mercies promised to David. If we come to God to serve Him, He will covenant with us to do us good and make our lives complete. God's covenant with us is an everlasting covenant—it is from everlasting and continues to everlasting.

Urgency of Seeking and Promise of Reward (Isa. 55:6–10)

Seek the LORD while he may be found (v. 6) is a wakeup call that should be a reminder to all that the invitation, by the very finiteness of life, will not last forever. Note that there are so many action words in this passage. *Seek*, *call*, and *turn* are all words that require us to do something. Repent! How can we continually ask the Lord for favor when, like the Israelites, we want to do it our way? The Lord required the Israelites to do something. They had to return to the place that God had given them. They had to turn, return, and be restored. **Call on him while he is near** (v. 6) means He is always near, waiting patiently for us to acknowledge our need and His presence. The danger is that there may come a time when we have pushed the Spirit away to the point that our hearts are hardened and can no longer hear the invitation.

WORDS FROM WESLEY

Isaiah 55:6

Seek—Labour to get the knowledge of God's will, and to obtain His grace and favour. *While*—In this day of grace, while He offers mercy and reconciliation. *Near*—Ready and desirous to receive you to mercy. (ENOT)

If we allow our hearts to be hardened, it is a certainty that at death and judgment the door will be shut (Luke 16:26; 13:25–26). Mercy is offered now, but then judgment without mercy will take place.

As we look toward God, Isaiah 55:8–9 reminds us that our thoughts and ways are not like God's. **As the heavens are higher than the earth, so are my ways higher than your ways and my thoughts than your thoughts** (v. 9). This is a reminder again to sinners and Christians alike that our thinking must not center only on earthly things. We need to forsake our evil ways and thoughts in order to bring them into compliance with His. The Israelites could not depend on themselves to find a place of restoration. God had to take them there. Sinners need to understand that they cannot count on works or possessions to secure a place in eternity. Only through God's grace and mercy are we offered the direction to restoration through Jesus Christ.

WORDS FROM WESLEY

Isaiah 55:8

For—If any man injure you, especially if he do it greatly and frequently, you are slow and backward to forgive him. But I am ready to forgive all penitents, how many, and great, and numberless soever their sins be. (ENOT)

The reference to watering the earth—**As the rain and the snow come down from heaven, and do not return to it without watering the earth and making it bud and flourish** (v. 10)— is a spiritual reminder that the seeds that are planted in our lives have to be watered and nourished in order to grow. Just as the land that sustained the Israelites had to rest during the Sabbath period (Lev. 26:34) in order to be replenished and be fruitful, our spirits must rest in the Lord so they can be restored and be productive. God's restoration is both physical and spiritual. This is where we get the term *sabbatical*. It means time off or vacation. Just as teachers and pastors take a sabbatical for rest or research, so do all of us need that time off periodically from the routines of our world.

Covenant Promise of God's Peace (Isa. 55:11–13)

Though our sins are many and we may backslide and are still prone to offend, God will continue to repeat His pardon and welcome even backsliding children who return to Him in sincerity.

So is my word that goes out from my mouth: It will not return to me empty, but will . . . achieve the purpose for which I sent it (v. 11). Even when it is the desire of our hearts to live a sanctified life, we are still able to stumble and fall. How wonderful that God's forgiveness is ongoing and repetitious! The Word that goes out of God's mouth is His messenger—Jesus. Once we have head and heart knowledge of who God is, when we have called to Him and sought Him, He will be found in us. Our hearts and voices shout out in praise. We have freedom from bondage, and we rejoice in our redemption. **The mountains and hills will burst into song before you, and all the trees of the field will clap their hands** (v. 12). The psalmist David wrote, "The hills are clothed with gladness. . . . The meadows are covered with flocks, and the valleys are mantled with grain; they shout for joy and sing" (Ps. 65:12–13).

Creation sings God's glory, and so should we. When a lost soul discovers the truth and has been set free, he or she should not hold back that praise. It should go directly up to the One whose ways and thoughts are higher than ours. Otherwise, trees and mountains will render praise in our place.

In place of sin, pain, and desolation, God will gift us with peace, joy, and righteousness. God has placed the everlasting sign of redemption on us, and Satan will never be able to destroy it (Isa. 55:13).

To those who have never responded to God's invitation to come and receive without cost, He says, "Give ear and come to me; hear me, that your soul may live" (v. 3). Enter into that everlasting covenant that promises eternal life with Jesus Christ in the heavenly realms.

DISCUSSION

It's thrilling to be invited to a special occasion or to meet a special person, but receiving an invitation from God is greater than all the rest.

1. Did you ever think you might die of thirst? If so, what was the occasion? How did it feel to have your thirst quenched?

2. Why can God justly offer to quench a sinner's spiritual thirst?

3. How might a person spend his or her labor on what doesn't satisfy?

4. Based on Jesus' conversation with a woman of Samaria (John 4:1–26), would you agree that no one is excluded from God's invitation to take the water of life? Explain.

5. Read Isaiah 55:6–7. Why do you think the instructions to seek and call precede the instructions to forsake wicked ways and evil thoughts?

6. Do you think God might withdraw His invitation from someone who repeatedly rejects it? Defend your answer.

7. How does it encourage you to know God's Word will not return to Him empty?

PRAYER

God, in this study, we've heard You call out for us to listen, repent, and respond. So we do what You ask. Today, we repent and invite You to speak, for Your servants are listening.

12

FREE AT LAST!

Isaiah 61:1–11

The year of the Lord's favor provides a framework for His church.

Who doesn't want to protect the air we breathe, water we drink, beauty of nature, and wonder of wildlife? However, most of us would agree that eco terrorists go too far when they sabotage logging efforts, blow up SUVs, set fire to ski resorts, and destroy millions of dollars' worth of property. Violating the law and putting human life at risk are ugly courses of action.

Believers understand that someday Jesus will execute righteousness on earth and restore the planet. Devastated places will become delightful places. He will energize the environment and make it enjoyable for all. This study increases our confidence in His ability to bestow "a crown of beauty instead of ashes" (Isa. 61:3).

COMMENTARY

Isaiah lived during the period of the divided kingdom of Israel. As a young man, he saw all of north Israel carried away by the Assyrians (734 B.C.). In 721 B.C., just thirteen years later, Samaria fell and the rest of the northern kingdom was carried away. Later, Assyria destroyed forty-six walled cities in Judah and carried away two hundred thousand captives. Then in 701 B.C., the Assyrians were stopped at the walls of Jerusalem through direct intervention by an angel of God. Isaiah lived his entire life under the threat of Assyrian power. In his lifetime, all of Israel and Judah, except Jerusalem, were ruined at the hands of the Assyrians.

The first thirty-nine chapters of Isaiah deal with God's judgment. Chapters 40–66 focus on comfort through God's grace. Chapter 61 is at the heart of this second section related to God's comfort. This portion of Isaiah's message brought hope and comfort to the people of Jerusalem, who had seen their nation collapse around them.

Like other prophetic writings, chapter 61 also has a message beyond the time in which it was written. Isaiah was convinced that Israel was to be a messianic nation to the world. He foresaw a day when a great and wonderful blessing from God would come to all nations through his nation. His writings are full of anticipation for when that day would come.

So there was a message for Israel in Isaiah's time, and there is a message for Christians in the church age. In a time when Israel had fallen and Jerusalem was nearly destroyed, Isaiah had a message of hope for people who would obey God. But in the long view, there is a message for twenty-first-century believers in his words as well.

1. Identity of the Messiah. There are qualities expressed here that describe the mission of the Messiah and aid us in identifying Him. There are many other prophecies about the Messiah that must be considered as well, but no one could be the Messiah unless He fulfilled this mission.

2. Insights into the nature of God. The Messiah was sent by God, and therefore, we gain insights into His nature by understanding the mission to which the Messiah was sent.

3. Implications for the church. For those who would follow the Messiah, an understanding of His mission in the world would indicate the kind of mission those followers must fulfill. The New Testament teaches us that God desires for us to be like His dear Son. Thus, our understanding of Jesus and the role He fulfilled implies the role we are to fulfill as His church.

Compassion for the Deprived (Isa. 61:1–3)

The Messiah would be **anointed** and **sent** to the **poor, brokenhearted, captives, prisoners,** and those **who mourn** and **grieve** (vv. 1–3). People disregarded the poor and meek, but He would lift them up (Matt. 5:3, 5). Brokenheartedness represents those who were in misery, despair, and hopelessness. This Anointed One would restore their future. He would provide deliverance to the captive and prisoner. Those who mourn would be comforted by Him (Matt. 5:4). The Messiah's ministry would be to people like those who heard these words from Isaiah.

WORDS FROM WESLEY
Isaiah 61:1

Upon me—Though the prophet may speak of himself, yet it is principally to be understood of Christ. *Anointed*—Set me apart, both capacitating Him with gifts, and commissioning Him with authority; and yet more, as it is applied to Christ, a power to make all effectual, from whence He hath also the name of Messiah among the Hebrews, and of Christ among the Greeks; nay Christ alone among the prophets hath obtained this name, Ps. 45:7. The prophet describes first, who Christ is, and then what are His offices. *Liberty*—This appertains to Christ's kingly office, whereby He proclaims liberty from the dominion of sin, and from the fear of hell. (ENOT)

The mission of the Messiah would be to transform the conditions of those who had been deprived of all they possessed. He would **bestow on them a crown of beauty instead of ashes** (Isa. 61:3). Ashes demonstrated total misery and despair, but a garland crown expressed happiness and joy. He would provide **the oil of gladness instead of mourning** (v. 3). When people mourned, they did not care about their appearances, but after mourning they would anoint themselves with oil to improve their appearances. They would be given **a garment of praise instead of a spirit of despair** (v. 3).

The transformation would be complete only when they were **called oaks of righteousness, a planting of the LORD for the display of his splendor** (v. 3). The tendency of the Israelites toward false gods, and the accompanying disregard for God's law, was the cause of God's judgment upon them. They would be transformed with a new name that identified them as being strong in His righteousness.

WORDS FROM WESLEY

Isaiah 61:3

Ashes—By ashes understand whatever is proper for days of mourning, as by beauty whatever may become times of rejoicing. *Oil of joy*—He calls it oil of joy in allusion to those anointings they were wont to use in times of joy, gladness for heaviness; and it is called a garment in allusion to their festival ornaments, for they had garments appropriated to their conditions, some suitable to times of rejoicing, and some to times of mourning. *Called*— That they may be so. *Trees*—That they shall be firm, solid, and well rooted, being by faith engrafted into Christ, and bringing forth fruit suitable to the soil wherein they are planted. (ENOT)

Jesus read these verses in Luke 4:18–19 and then used them to identify himself as the Messiah in Luke 4:21. John the Baptist sent men to ask Him, "Are you the one who was to come, or should we expect someone else?" Jesus replied, "Go back and report to John what you have seen and heard: The blind receive sight, the lame walk, those who have leprosy are cured, the deaf hear, the dead are raised, and the good news is preached to the poor" (Luke 7:20, 22).

Those who would follow Jesus would do well to remember this central aspect of Jesus' role as the Messiah.

Restoration for the Devastated (Isa. 61:4–6)

Isaiah and the people he spoke to certainly understood the concept of devastation. The only part of their country that remained was Jerusalem. Imagine that during your lifetime your nation was completely destroyed except for a few states or provinces. Then by the time you are old, all that is left is your nation's capital, and it has been threatened directly. That is the kind of devastation Isaiah had witnessed in his homeland.

As Isaiah perceived the work of the Messiah, he saw a time when that which was devastated would be restored. His vision of that restoration was communicated as a physical rebuilding of the area destroyed by the Assyrians, a very understandable and welcomed concept to the people of Israel and Judah. The Messiah's work would be one of rebuilding and restoration.

The New Testament also depicts the people of God as being builders (1 Cor. 3:9–11; Eph. 2:20–22; 1 Pet. 2:5). The restoration is being built upon the foundation laid by Jesus Christ. It is a spiritual building that will culminate in the heavenly kingdom. Jesus Christ and His followers work to rebuild what has been devastated by generations of sin.

In Isaiah 61:6, the picture switches from building to ministry. Each of God's people will be **priests of the LORD and named ministers of our God** (v. 6). Peter spoke of the fulfillment of this ministry of restoration in 1 Peter 2:9–10. The effects of this restoration are not limited to one group of people or one area of the world.

WORDS FROM WESLEY

Isaiah 61:6

The priests—The whole body of them shall now be as near to God as the priests were formerly, and shall be a royal priesthood. This is most certainly true of all the faithful under the gospel. (ENOT)

Inheritance for the Disgraced (Isa. 61:7–9)

Israel and Judah had been shamed and disgraced at the hands of the Assyrians. To be without an inheritance or to have nothing left to pass on in an estate was a shameful and disgraceful thing for them. But **instead of their shame** and **disgrace** (v. 7), God would provide an inheritance for them.

To emphasize in dramatic form the inheritance that was in store, Isaiah used word associations in verse 7. In the first part of the verse, **double portion** is associated with what they will **receive**, and **rejoice** is associated with their **inheritance**. In the second portion of the verse, they **inherit a double portion** and they will possess (receive) **joy**. Not only will that which is lost be restored, but more than is expected will be inherited. The accompanying joy will be beyond expectation as well. Isaiah spoke of a time when the shame and disgrace associated with our sins would be removed and we would receive a greater inheritance and joy beyond description (1 Pet. 1:3–4, 8–9).

God gave His reason and purpose for that which Isaiah saw for the future. **I, the LORD, love justice; I hate robbery and iniquity** (Isa. 61:8). In His **faithfulness**, God promised to **reward** those who live in true relationship with Him with **an everlasting covenant** (v. 8). This reward is greater than the restoration of land in this world that is bound by time and will come to an end. It is a covenant that will be a reward that has no end. These true people of God **will be known among the nations and . . . peoples** as a people that **the LORD has blessed** (v. 9).

The restoration and inheritance that are promised are based on the attributes of God. God loves justice. He will reward those who stand for justice and against robbery and iniquity. God is faithful. He will not abandon His people in their time of need. He is eternal. Only an eternal being can enter into an everlasting covenant. The attributes of God form the foundation and secure the promises Isaiah described. People who place their faith in

Jesus Christ are the descendants of Israel who receive these promises.

Salvation for the Defiled (Isa. 61:10–11)

These final verses look to a time of **delight** (v. 10) and rejoicing, when all that has been promised is fulfilled. Those who have been defiled by sin are **clothed . . . with garments of salvation** (v. 10). Those garments of salvation are like a **bridegroom** who **adorns his head like a priest** (v. 10). The priest offers the sacrifice of blood for redemption of the one making the offering. They are **arrayed . . . in a robe of righteousness** worn as a **bride adorns herself with her jewels** (v. 10).

In the New Testament, the church is called the bride of Christ (Eph. 5:25). At the end of time, the culmination of this eternal covenant will take place at the wedding of the Lamb. "Let us rejoice and be glad and give him glory! For the wedding of the Lamb has come, and his bride has made herself ready. Fine linen, bright and clean, was given her to wear. (Fine linen stands for the righteous acts of the saints)" (Rev. 19:7–8).

WORDS FROM WESLEY
Isaiah 61:11

Righteousness—His great work of salvation shall break out and appear. *Praise*—As the natural product, and fruit of it. (ENOT)

Righteousness and praise will **spring up** (Isa. 61:11) like plants bursting through the soil in springtime. It will grow in the **soil** of God's grace **garden** until the time of the eternal harvest, when the final harvest reveals the abundance of God's crop of salvation.

The Messiah will replace ashes, mourning, and despair with a crown of beauty, oil of gladness, and a garment of praise. This will come to pass as those who have been devastated experience restoration and rebuilding. They will become priests of the Lord and ministers of God. Not only will that which has been lost be restored, but they will receive an inheritance that is beyond expectation, accompanied by inexpressible and glorious joy. These promises are assured because of the righteousness, holiness, and faithfulness of God.

The message of this passage goes far beyond restoration of land to Israel and Judah, but involves an everlasting covenant with God. Delight and joy are experienced through the eternal salvation and righteousness provided by the Messiah. The groom (Messiah) and bride (the church) are adorned for the great wedding celebration. An eternal harvest of righteousness and praise will be experienced by those who receive the Messiah's salvation. That which was destroyed by sin is restored in the everlasting covenant of God's salvation. Shame and disgrace are replaced with an abundant inheritance of salvation. While we are in this world, it is the work of the church to proclaim this salvation to the deprived, devastated, disgraced, and defiled.

Paul summed it up in his prayer for the believers in Ephesus: "I pray also that the eyes of your heart may be enlightened in order that you may know the hope to which he has called you, the riches of his glorious inheritance in the saints" (Eph. 1:18).

DISCUSSION

Isaiah's message focused on the Messiah. It was good news of hope and comfort.

1. What can the gospel do for the brokenhearted and for those who are in bondage to sin?

2. How does knowing you are commissioned by the Sovereign Lord motivate you to share the good news of Jesus?

3. Do you believe the predictions in Isaiah 61:4–6 will have a literal or symbolic fulfillment? Defend your answer.

4. Why do you agree or disagree that secular society demeans Christians?

5. According to Ephesians 5:25 and Revelation 19:7–8, what joyful event awaits Christians? How soon do you think this event will take place? Defend your answer.

6. What customary preparations does a bride make for her wedding? How should the bride of Christ, the church, prepare for its wedding?

7. What major differences do you see between the character of nations now and their future character when Jesus restores our planet?

PRAYER

Father in heaven, in these glimpses of Your Son's ministry, we gain a new understanding of our role in Your work on earth. Equip us for ministry. Keep us looking toward the inheritance You're holding safely in heaven for us.

WORDS FROM WESLEY WORKS CITED

ENOT: Wesley, J. (1765). *Explanatory Notes upon the Old Testament* (Vol. 1–3). Bristol: William Pine.

JJW: *The Journal of the Rev. John Wesley, A.M*. Standard. Edited by Nehemiah Curnock. 8 vols. London: Robert Culley, Charles H. Kelley, 1909–1916.

PW: *The Poetical Works of John and Charles Wesley*. Edited by D. D. G. Osborn. 13 vols. London: Wesleyan-Methodist Conference Office, 1868.

WJW: *The Works of John Wesley*. Third Edition, Complete and Unabridged. 14 vols. London: Wesleyan Methodist Book Room, 1872.

OTHER BOOKS IN THE
WESLEY BIBLE STUDIES SERIES

Genesis
Exodus
Leviticus through Deuteronomy (available May 2015)
Joshua through Ruth (available May 2015)
1 Samuel through 2 Chronicles
Ezra through Esther
Job through Song of Songs
Isaiah
Jeremiah through Daniel
Hosea through Malachi (available May 2015)
Matthew
Mark
Luke
John
Acts
Romans
1–2 Corinthians
Galatians through Colossians and Philemon
1–2 Thessalonians
1 Timothy through Titus
Hebrews
James
1–2 Peter and Jude
1–3 John
Revelation

Now Available in the Wesley Bible Studies Series

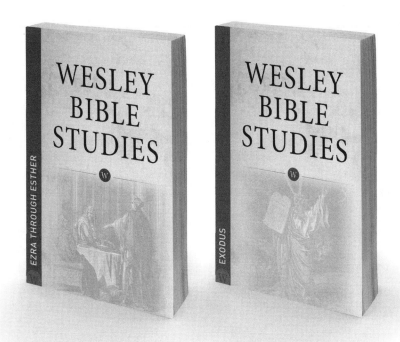

Each book in the Wesley Bible Studies series provides a thoughtful and powerful survey of key Scriptures in one or more biblical books. They combine accessible commentary from contemporary teachers, with relevantly highlighted direct quotes from the complete writings and life experiences of John Wesley, along with the poetry and hymns of his brother Charles. For each study, creative and engaging questions foster deeper fellowship and growth.

Ezra through Esther
978-0-89827-842-2
978-0-89827-843-9 (e-book)

Exodus
978-0-89827-850-7
978-0-89827-851-4 (e-book)